"THIS IS A BOOK on education at all stages of life—the art of learning, growing, and becoming. Its focus is on continuing education—learning co-extensive with life. It deals with self-education—the key to continuing learning. Its concern is with liberal education—the development and use of the mind, and the cultivation of intellectual interests as they affect the nature and quality of human life."—*from the Preface*

THIS VOLUME OF ESSAYS on education is addressed to the general reader. Young and old, those in and out of school, will find this a book that will change their lives for the better. The author draws on a lifetime of reading and reflection to apply the power of positive thinking to the problem of intellectual growth.

THE ADVENTURE OF LEARNING

THE ADVENTURE
OF LEARNING

WILLIAM PEARSON TOLLEY
Chancellor Emeritus
Syracuse University

 SYRACUSE UNIVERSITY PRESS   1977

Copyright © 1977 by Syracuse University Press
Syracuse, New York 13210

All Rights Reserved

First Edition
Second Printing, 1977

Library of Congress Cataloging in Publication Data

Tolley, William Pearson, 1900–
   The adventure of learning.

   Includes bibliographical references and index.
    1. Education—1965–   2. Self-culture.
I. Title.
LA132.T64   370   77-21652
ISBN 0-8156-0142-5

Manufactured in the United States of America

For
    Jonathan
        Debra
            Jennifer
                David
                    Paul
                        Neil
                           Sara
                           and
                             Lael

PREFACE

THIS IS A BOOK on education at all stages of life—the art of learning, growing, and becoming. Its focus is on continuing education—learning co-extensive with life. It deals with self-education—the key to continuing learning. Its concern is with liberal education—the development and use of the mind and the cultivation of intellectual interests as they affect the nature and quality of human life.

This book is addressed to people of all ages. Education is too important to be reserved for and restricted to the young. It is an opportunity for all, from the youngest to the oldest. To live life to the full we must learn all we can as long as we can.

In our day of institutionalized learning we almost always think of education as organized instruction. We define it in terms of teachers, classes, and courses. It is structured learning, and we work for certificates, credits, and degrees. We do not give equal attention to the unlimited possibilities of self-improvement through self-education. This is especially true in education in the liberal arts. When we do think of

self-education it is likely to be in the cultivation of our hob-
bies, our recreational interests, or in our technical, vocational,
or professional development.

There are many books addressed to the do-it-yourself
carpenter and mechanic. There are few addressed to the bright
and curious literate who needs encouragement to continue his
or her acquaintance with the liberal arts. To be sure, there is
nothing new about the neglect of liberal learning in the years
after the completion of our formal schooling. This has been a
problem in every age. What is new, however, is the current
neglect of liberal learning in the curriculum of our schools and
colleges. With the widespread abandonment of classical learning a large part of what we have called liberal education will
remain unknown unless we discover and learn it by and for
ourselves.

The important question, of course, is our attention to
the development and use of the mind. It may be an exaggeration to say that no space on earth is so undeveloped as the
space between human ears. It is not an exaggeration to say
that the mind of man is shockingly under-utilized and underdeveloped. In the use of the mind we are only fractionally productive. We all reach the limits of our physical strength and
those of our nervous system, but we rarely use the full power
of our minds. Here perhaps is our greatest undeveloped
resource.

The increasing participation in athletics by people of
all ages is an encouraging sign. Soon we hope it will be
matched by a like participation in intellectual and cultural activities. When that occurs perhaps Western society will be
both civilized and affluent. The increasing leisure that so often
brings with it ennui and discontent should also enrich life. It is

an unparalleled opportunity to redirect our interests and re-define our values.

Bernard of Chartres is known to students of the Middle Ages by his statement: "We are like dwarfs that sit on the shoulders of giants; hence we see more and further than they, yet not by reason of the keenness of our vision nor the outstanding stature of our bodies, but because we have been raised aloft and are being carried by these men of giant dimensions."[1]

In Bernard's day there was perhaps an excessive reverence for the past, but today the reverse is true. Our debt to the past is largely ignored, yet we still need to sit on the shoulders of giants. Their numbers are legion. It is the view from their shoulders that we should see.

I should like to express my thanks to Chancellor Melvin A. Eggers and the Trustees of Syracuse University for permission to use material from *The Transcendent Aim*, a volume of my addresses edited by Dr. Frank P. Piskor and published by Syracuse University in 1967.

I also thank Mrs. Dorothy Sickels and Mrs. Elizabeth Mozley for their encouragement and assistance.

In the close and happy association with students and colleagues at Drew, Allegheny, and Syracuse, learning was

1. *Twelfth Century Europe and the Foundations of Modern Society*, edited by Marshall Claggett, Gaines Post, and Robert Reynolds. *The School of Chartres*, Raymond Klibansky (Madison: University of Wisconsin Press, 1966), p. 5.

never impersonal. It was not a station-to-station call, but person to person. Learning is an intimate personal experience. Teachers are enormously important. Even so, no one can learn for us. We must discover for ourselves the excitement and joy of learning. The experience is ours. Learning is our adventure.

Syracuse, New York   WILLIAM PEARSON TOLLEY
Spring 1977

CONTENTS

THE ADVENTURE OF LEARNING

Visibility Unlimited

I N *Listen! the Wind* Anne Morrow Lindbergh tells of problems with wind and weather before flying from Africa to South America and of the special meaning of the report from the Weather Bureau, "Visibility Unlimited." "At the word *unlimited*, I looked up," she tells us. "Lovely word, which opens like a window from the straight walls of a radio report. . . . *Unlimited*, my breath quickens at the sound of it. For it suggests more than the technically perfect, 'ceiling and visibility unlimited.' It calls up pictures of a soft wide cloudless sky, the morning of an endless summer day, a smooth and rippleless sea, spread silken to the horizon."[1]

The weather report for the adventure of learning is also "Visibility Unlimited." Learning is not only "ceiling and visibility unlimited," but boundless, unlimited opportunity. In our journey through the endless horizons of space and time and thought we are limited only by the brevity or length of our life span and the development of our special aptitudes and powers.

1. Anne Morrow Lindbergh, *Listen! the Wind* (New York: Harcourt, Brace and Company, 1938), pp. 239–40.

Education is not a right. It is not something we are given whether we want it or not. It is not a key to wealth or a guarantee of success. It is an opportunity for growth. It is the art of becoming in emotional maturity, health, and physical fitness, in spiritual insight and religious faith, character, and integrity, and in knowledge and wisdom.

To be sure, we need a travel plan. Neither our time nor our energy is unlimited. We cannot go everywhere at once in foreign travel, and this is equally true in the experience of learning. We must select what we shall study first. The choice is important: it should be something we really want to learn. Over and beyond the pleasure of learning it should serve us in the future. Not only should learning take us somewhere, but it should allow us later to go farther more easily.

One of the defects of our schools and colleges is that we study too many subjects. On the whole it is better to study one subject in continuity and depth, than to know a little about so many. Our first goal should be to have a sense of what knowledge is in at least one field of inquiry. We should know its relationships and connections. We should know its structure. We should learn its principles. We should understand its general ideas.

Before we begin, however, we may find that the first problem to solve is the use of time. Nothing is studied so little. Nothing is wasted so much. We all have more time than we need. As a rule, the busiest and most productive people are relaxed and at ease, not at all tense, hurried, or driven. They are alert and attentive. They try to get to the heart of an issue. They do not give the impression, however, that they are racing against time. They are well organized. They plan their time. They manage time; time does not manage them.

If time is a problem, one obvious place to begin is to take a look at the hours we spend reading the daily newspapers. If we will clock ourselves for seven days we shall be shocked and surprised! While we are about it we might also time the hours spent listening to radio and television. We shall have plenty of time once we begin to use it more carefully.

After our setting-up exercises are behind us as we begin the day let us try reading for twenty minutes or more from a carefully chosen book. We should do this before we open the morning newspaper. The same rule might be followed when we get home at night. Some people prefer to read one book at a time. Many of us, however, find that we read far more by turning from one book to another in the course of an evening or day. This may mean that some books are savoured, others are tasted and put aside, others are read quickly, and still others are read again and again. This also permits us to indulge an interest in poetry, while also reading plays, fiction, and current non-fiction.

One of the best incentives to reading is to keep at least one book we are reading in each room of the apartment or house. This allows us to take advantage of odd minutes to read. This is important. Gains in learning productivity are impressive when time formerly wasted in waiting for friends and members of the family becomes reading time. When more evenings and weekends also become reading time, the gains are even more remarkable. For those who travel a great deal there should always be a good book to read. The time spent waiting in airports is a reading opportunity we should make the most of. It is not a bad rule to read three old books for each new one. The rate of non-fiction to fiction may be different when we are on a holiday,[2] but for the rest of the year it should be at least ten to one. Whether non-fiction or fiction, we do not need to read many of the best sellers. We should choose books by their importance, not by their date of publication.[3]

Most people go through life without planning their reading. Few things, however, will make a greater difference. If financial planning is important, the planning of our learning program is of equal importance. We need both long- and short-range plans. We also need to distinguish between vocational objectives and learning for self-improvement.

In the absence of a reading program we might start by reading the Bible. Reading it from cover to cover is always a rewarding experience, no matter how many times we have done it before. A second choice would be to read the Greek tragedies and comedies. There are many excellent translations available. Reading them will give great pleasure in the long winter evenings and hasten the coming of spring.

Unless we have chosen our field of intellectual inquiry and are limiting our reading to it, we should have a program of general reading in which we begin with one author at a time. In one year the reading program may be Shakespeare. A second year it might be Plato and Aristotle. Over the months and years one may move from Dante to Chaucer; from Francis Bacon to Locke, Berkeley, and Hume; from Stevenson to

2. But Emerson, in his *English Traits* (Boston: Phillips, Sampson, 1856), reminds us that "Classics which at home are drowsily read have a strange charm in a country inn, or in the transom of a merchant brig" (p. 37).

3. In his *Society and Solitude* (Boston: Houghton Mifflin, 1904), Emerson says, "Never read any book that is not a year old" (Vol. VII, p. 96).

Kipling and George Bernard Shaw; from Kant to Hegel; from Thoreau to Whitman; from Henri Bergson to William James; from Jane Austen to George Eliot; from Anthony Trollope to Henry James; from Milton to William Cowper; from Corneille to Moliere and Racine; from Montagne to Voltaire and Rousseau; from Victor Hugo to Balzac and Dumas; from Samuel Pepys to Samuel Johnson; from Coleridge and Wordsworth to Browning, Tennyson, and Keats; from Emily Dickinson to Robert Frost; from Thackeray to Dickens; from Augustine to Anselm; from Isocrates to Quintilian; from Peter Abelard to Thomas Aquinas; from Herodotus to Plutarch and Thucydides; from Homer to Virgil; and not to forget Cervantes, Tolstoi, and John Wolfgang von Goethe. There are ten thousand choices! You may reply, "Yes, but there is only one life." Agreed, but we shall be pleasantly surprised at how much we shall read if we have a plan and follow it.

What we have been talking about is not a reading program that advances us vocationally or professionally. We need a program for that, too. Nor are we thinking of books on current affairs, books on the theater, politics, economics, history, and poetry. We do not need a plan for them, although we should make a place for them. Nor do we need a plan for trade and professional magazines. We are concerned here with important books that will not only give us pleasure but will feed the mind and build our structure of knowledge and culture. We may think we are too busy, but we are not. If we make use of minutes and hours now wasted we shall find the time.

In the absence of teachers we shall do our own reading and our own thinking. We shall find it necessary, however, to make constant use of reference books, textbooks, and books

by authorities in the field. We may not agree with the authorities, but they will teach us much. They will be particularly
helpful in showing us what to look for and in pointing out
strengths or weaknesses that we had failed to note or evaluate.
Let us get all the help we can. We need contact with other
minds, and the more the better.

For most of us there are great areas of our brain which
lie dormant all our lives. We develop only a fraction of our
intellectual powers. It is clear that for all of at least normal
intelligence our sights are much too low. This is particularly
true for those of high intelligence. In our growth in knowledge
and intellectual power we have endless opportunity.

"The Vedas say," Thoreau tells us,

"all intelligences awake with the morning." To him,
whose elastic and vigorous thought keeps pace with the
sun, the day is a perpetual morning. It matters not what
the clocks say. Morning is when I am awake and there
is a dawn in me. Moral reform is the effort to throw off
sleep. The millions are awake enough for physical labor;
but only one in a million is awake enough for effective
intellectual exertion, only one in a hundred millions to a
poetic or divine life. To be awake is to be alive. I have
never yet met a man who was quite awake. . . . We
must learn to reawaken and keep ourselves awake, not
by mechanical means, but by an infinite expectation of
the dawn, which does not forsake us in our soundest
sleep.[4]

4. Henry David Thoreau, *Walden and Civil Disobedience* (Boston: Houghton Mifflin, 1957), Chapter 2, p. 62.

The message of Thoreau is: Open your eyes! Awake and live!

Spinoza sums up our feeling about the rewards of learning: "But love toward a thing eternal and infinite, feeds the mind wholly with joy, and is itself unmingled with any sadness, wherefore it is greatly to be desired and sought for with all our strength."[5]

Yes, learning is opportunity. With it we have horizons unlimited. It calls to mind that "merchant man, seeking good pearls: who when he had found one pearl of great price, went and sold all that he had, and bought it."[6]

5. Baruch de Spinoza, *On the Improvement of the Understanding*, translated by R. H. M. Elwes (New York: Willey Book Co. 1901), p. 3.

6. Matthew 13:45–46.

2

Education is a Solo Flight

To DARE to do what has not been done, to do what appears to be impossible, is the spirit of modern man. To build a new heaven and a new earth has been man's dream in every age, but especially in this century.

It is not the cynic, the timid, or the faint-hearted who ushers in a new day. It is the man of ideas and action, it is the inventor, the scientist, the creator, the builder, and the leader. Not all the old answers are final. To continue our progress we must find fresh approaches and new ways. We must also test the proposed answers. In the new world of science and technology knowledge is power and power is knowledge.

In the endless tales of gods and heroes that have come down to us from ancient Greece, few are better known than the story of Daedalus and Icarus. The place is the island of Crete, with its remarkable civilization and its immense wealth and power. The time is about 1400 B.C., when Minoan culture and influence were at their zenith. Despite this early date, Daedalus and Icarus are modern in outlook and thought. They would be at home in the most modern of times.

Daedalus is said to be the architect who designed the famous Labyrinth for the Minotaur in Crete, and who showed Ariadne how Theseus could escape from it. With the exception of Prometheus he is perhaps the best example in Greek mythology of the power of creative thought.

For Daedalus nothing is too difficult. King Minos imprisons Daedalus and Icarus in a tower, but they manage to escape. King Minos cannot find their hiding place, but to prevent them leaving by sea has every ship searched before it is permitted to sail. Daedalus, however, does not admit defeat. He tells his son Icarus that escape may be checked by water and by land, but the air and the sky are free. Putting his mind to work he proposes the boldest of means to escape—to fashion wings and fly.

The story of Daedalus and Icarus suggests that new knowledge is not without danger, and that even in daring greatly there is a place for caution and a need for all the wisdom and experience we can muster. The legend tells us something about the power of an idea and the importance of a goal. And finally it reminds us that if we want to fly we must try our own wings.

Icarus was just a boy. He was of little help to his father in the design and fashioning of the wings. He

> Stood by and watched and raising his shiny face
> To let a feather, light as down, fall on it,
> Or stuck his thumb into the yellow wax,
> Fooling around, the way a boy will, always,
> Whenever a father tries to get some work done.[1]

1. Ovid, *Metamorphoses*, translated by Rolfe Humphries (Bloomington, Ind.: Indiana University Press, 1955), pp. 187–88.

Finally the wings are made, and Daedalus gives careful instructions as to their use. The mind of Icarus, however, is on other things.

You remember Daedalus says:

> I warn you, Icarus, fly a middle course:
> Don't go too low, or water will weight the wings down;
> Don't go too high, or the sun's fire will burn them.
> Keep to the middle way. And one more thing,
> No fancy steering by star or constellation.
> Follow my lead![2]

Daedalus was a man of wide experience. He was skilled in many trades. He had survived many close calls. He was crafty and shrewd and resourceful. He tries to tell Icarus all that he knows about flying.

It is not easy, however, to learn from the knowledge and experience of others. In this case Icarus is not really listening. So when he tries his new wings he cannot remember his instructions. It is, however, great fun to fly. It is so exhilarating and gives him such a heady sense of power that he feels he needs no direction or help. He is so turned on that he is sure he has achieved instant wisdom and experience. Until he falls he is really on a trip.

"Keep on, Keep on," signals Daedalus, "follow me." He guides him in flight and the wings move.[3]

> And the boy
> Thought *This is wonderful!* and left his father,

2. Ibid., p. 188.

3. Ibid.

Soared higher, higher, drawn to the vast heaven.
Nearer the sun, the wax that held the wings
Melted in that fierce heat, and the bare arms
Beat up and down in air, and lacking oarage
Took hold of nothing. *Father!* he cried, and *Father!*
Until the blue sea hushed him, the dark water
Men call the Icarian now.[4]

We miss some of the significance of the legend if we focus all our attention on Icarus. We need to remember that as Apollodorus tells the story Daedalus flew successfully to Sicily where he was given sanctuary by King Cocalus. He even had the last laugh on Minos, who was killed in a vain attempt to recapture him.

It was an unheard-of achievement. It required planning, daring, faith, knowledge, experience, and just the right measure of caution. Most of all, however, it required an idea—the idea of man-made wings to fly. This was the first and most important requirement. This was the beginning of the invention. Every invention starts with an idea—the steam engine, the motor-driven ship, the typewriter, the automobile, the telephone. The forecasting of invention is an integral part of the process of invention. The first and principal step is the concept. When we have set our goals and know where we are going, we have made an important start. Provided we are willing to work at it, we are well on our way.

When young Edward Blyth, who had such a seminal influence on Darwin, published a paper in 1835 (twenty-four years before the publication of *The Origin of Species*), dwelling at some length upon artificial selection and applying the

4. Ibid., Book VIII, pp. 188–89.

principle to wild nature, he could not have foreseen the influence of that principle. He was aware, however, that he had a new idea that flew in the face of accepted opinion. His second paper in 1837 reflects the progress made in his studies. Meditating upon adaptations and selection he asks, "to what extent may not the same take place in wild nature? May not then, a large proportion of what are considered species have descended from a common parentage?"[5] The framing of the question was itself a step toward the answer so definitively given by Darwin.

Albert Einstein was regarded by influential friends as a young man who might make his mark in physics if he would stop wasting his time on the problem of relativity, on which he had published a paper in 1905. Einstein, however, would not stop. He had an idea and he was sure he could work it out. Unable to find an academic position he took a post in the patent office at Berne, Switzerland. But he continued his studies. Using his spare time to advantage he made such great progress that he was made a Professor at Zurich in 1909. In 1916 he published his general "Theory of Relativity" and won instant recognition as a scientist of genius. In the beginning is the idea!

Finally, the story of Daedalus and Icarus suggests for all the risk if we would fly we must use our own wings. This is not to minimize the importance of good instruction. It is simply to point out that there is a limit to what the teacher can do. Good instruction can make a critical difference. On the other hand, no one can make the solo flight for us. No one

5. Quoted by Loren Eisley, *All the Strange Hours* (New York: Scribner's, 1975), p. 198.

can learn for us. Learning, like flying, is a direct personal experience. We must do it for ourselves.

Recently I had a chastening but instructive experience that underscores this. For a part of each summer, for many years, we have been going to the Thirty Thousand Island region of Georgian Bay in Lake Huron. There are no roads to our camp so we either fly in or go by boat. Finally we acquired a large enough boat to make the trip by ourselves. Believe it or not, however, first I had to learn the way! For all the many trips in which I had been a passenger, I did not know the channels. I learned them only by piloting our own boat.

Apparently one can be a passenger forever and learn nothing. Learning is active, not passive. It has to be our experience. The markers are there but we do not see them. We have been told about the shoals and the other dangers, but they are only words. We hear and see only when the responsibility and the experience is ours—when we do it for ourselves.

With the enormous expansion of public education we tend to identify learning with schooling. Education has come to mean organized learning in a classroom with other students under the supervision and instruction of a trained teacher. In America we have overdone it. We need to be reminded of the learning we can do by ourselves.

First of all, we should be reminded of the learning children can do before their formal schooling begins. In his autobiography, *All the Strange Hours*, Loren Eisley tells us:

> I did not have to go to kindergarten to learn to read. I
> had already mastered the alphabet at some earlier point.
> I had little primers of my own. The see-John-run sort of

thing or its equivalent in the year 1912. Yes, in that fashion I could read. Sometime in the months that followed, my elder brother paid a brief visit home. He brought with him a full adult version of Robinson Crusoe. He proceeded to read it to me in spare moments. I lived for that story. I hung upon my brother's words. Then abruptly, as was always happening in the world above me in the lamp-light, my brother had departed. We had reached only as far as the discovery of the foot print on the shore.

He left me the book, to be exact, but not a reader. I never asked Mother to read because her voice distressed me. Her inability to hear had made it harsh and jangling. My father read with great grace and beauty but he worked the long and dreadful hours of those years. There was only one thing evident to me. I had to get on with it, do it myself, otherwise I would never learn what happened to Crusoe.

I took DeFoe's book and some little inadequate dictionary I found about the house and proceeded to worry and chew my way like a puppy through the remaining pages. No doubt I lost the sense of a word here and there, but I had read it on my own. Papa bought me *Twenty Thousand Leagues Under the Sea* as a reward. I read that too. I began to read everything I could lay my hands on.[6]

Second, we can learn despite limited schooling. Benjamin Franklin, to cite one example, had but two years of attendance at school. At the age of eight he was sent to the grammar school in Boston Common where he rose to the head

6. Ibid., pp. 172–73.

of his class. After a year there he was sent to George Brownell's Academy. Benjamin failed arithmetic and at the end of the year was brought home at the age of ten to work in his father's business of candle-making and the boiling of soap. That experience was not a happy one, and Benjamin was soon apprenticed to his brother James to learn the printing business.

Ashamed of his ignorance of mathematics and knowing his formal schooling was over, he tells us:

> I took Cocker's Book of arithmetic and went thro' the whole of it by myself with great ease. I also read Seller's and Sturmy's Books of Navigation, and became acquainted with the little geometry they contain but never proceeded far in that science. I read about This Time Locke on Human Understanding and The Art of Thinking by Messrs. du Port Royal.
>
> While I was intent on improving my language, I met with an English grammar (I think it was Greenwood's) at the end of which there were two little sketches of The Arts of Rhetoric and Logic, the latter finishing with a specimen of a dispute in the Socratic Method. And soon after I procured Xenophon's Memorable Things of Socrates wherein there are many instances of the same method. I was charm'd with it, adopted it, dropt my abrupt contradiction and positive argumentation and put on the humble enquirer and doubter.[7]

The examples are legion, but in our time President Harry Truman, who could not afford to go to college, tells

---

7. Catherine Drinker Bowen, *The Most Dangerous Man in America* (Boston: Little, Brown, 1974), p. 17.

us how he became such a well-informed man. "I always had my nose stuck in a book," he tells us, "a history book mostly. Of course, the main reason you read a book is to get a better insight into the people you're talking to. There were about three thousand books in the library downtown, and I guess I read them all, including the encyclopedias. I'm embarrassed to say that I remembered what I read too."[8]

Finally, we need to be reminded that it is never too late to learn. It may be true that one cannot teach an old dog new tricks. One can, however, teach new tricks to a person, provided he or she is willing to learn. Indeed, we can teach ourselves. We may not learn as rapidly as we once did. Our memory at age seventy-five is not as reliable or as retentive as it was at forty. It may also require greater patience, persistence, and effort of will. Nonetheless, it is well within our power. At any age we can learn whatever we want to study.

There are late bloomers in life as well as in school and college. Immanuel Kant might not have been given tenure as a teacher in an American college. His development as a philosopher and scholar was so slow that he was forty-six before he was promoted to a professorship at a University of Konigsberg.[9] His book *The Critique of Pure Reason* was published when he was fifty-seven. He was sixty-six when he published his *Critique of Judgment,* and age sixty-nine when he wrote *Religion within the Limits of Pure Reason.* At seventy he published a little essay, "On the Power of the Mind to

8. Merle Miller, *Plain Speaking, an Oral Biography of Harry S. Truman* (New York: Berkley, 1973), p. 24.

9. He could have been named a Professor of Poetry at age forty but he declined. At forty-two he was appointed Assistant Librarian.

Master the Feeling of Illness by Force of Resolution." After retiring at seventy-two he wrote *The Metaphysics of Ethics* at age seventy-three and *Anthropology with Reference to Pragmatic Ends* at age seventy-four.[10]

Undiminished intellectual power is much less exceptional than we commonly think. Minds are made to be used. They are kept sharp by use. Ida Tarbell, Eleanor Roosevelt, Konrad Adenauer, Artur Rubenstein, Madame Curie, Edith Hamilton, Malvina Hoffman, Agnes Meyer, Anna Hyatt Huntington, Robert Frost, Sidney Hook, Samuel Eliot Morison, Bertrand Russell, Averell Harriman, George Bernard Shaw, Dean Acheson, Herbert Hoover, Winston Churchill, Justice Holmes, and Justice Cardozo are but names selected at random from a procession that is endless of men and women of formidable intellectual powers despite advanced age. In a day when men of seventy are still playing tennis and golf they can also exercise their minds. Since they can learn, they should. So rich and great an opportunity should not be missed.

Toward the end of the life of Diogenes of Sinope a friend said, "Diogenes, you are no longer young. Slow down now and rest a bit." To this Diogenes replied, "You would not give this advice to a runner in a race. Should you not say, 'Now for the first time you can see the goal, you should quicken your pace for a triumphant finish.' "[11]

But let us return to Daedalus and Icarus. With all respect to Greek mythology the idea of flying was probably

10. His book *On Education* was published in 1803, the year before his death, and consisted of notes he had recorded for many years as a teacher.

11. *Diogenes Laertius*, translated by R. D. Hicks (New York: G. P. Putnam and Son, 1925), Vol. II, Book VI, pp. 34–35.

not original with Daedalus. It had been around a long time. The earliest anthropoids, watching birds in flight, probably found themselves wishing for their own wings and wondering how they could be devised. In the absence of books ancient peoples had to rely on memory. Daedalus was heir to the oral traditions. They were the stories and the knowledge handed down from one generation to another and passed by travellers from country to country and people to people. The knowledge transmitted in this way was very considerable.

What distinguished Daedalus and Icarus from their fellows was that in the legend, at least, they took the idea and did something about it. For them, as for the Wright Brothers, the idea was not something merely to be talked about or wished for. It was not an inert idea, lying almost forgotten in the mind. It was a problem to be attacked. The idea of flying came alive by inquiry, direct observation, reflection, experimentation, analysis, and testing. Daedalus and Icarus provide and example of what happens when minds are active and knowledge is utilized.

Today, given an idea, the sensible thing is to go to the library and the laboratory. Both have their place. Not all originality comes from reading, but much of it does. At a time when knowledge multiplies so rapidly, reading the literature is one of the necessary first steps. But whether dealing with journals, books, or test tubes, what is required above all is an active, probing, searching mind. Learning is something we do for ourselves. Instruction is important. Experience and the voice of caution have their value. The adventure, however, is ours. The responsibility is ours. The thinking is ours. The excitement is ours. Education is a solo flight.

3

When Men and Mountains Meet

ONE OF THE MAJOR PROBLEMS we face in education is lighting the fires of intellectual curiosity and inquiry. As a rule it is not the absence of brain power that causes failure, but the absence of interest, intellectual hunger, motivation, drive, and desire. Winston Churchill, who was certainly not stupid, tells us that as a boy "where my reason, imagination, or interest were not engaged I would not or could not learn."[1]

Interest appears to be a particular problem in the so-called cultural subjects. This may be due in part to what Russell Davenport called "the American tendency to externalize all human values." As Davenport puts it:

> Our realistic toys, the remarks of our parents about the neighbor's new automobile, the urge that animates everyone we know to acquire more . . . all this profoundly orients us to a definition of happiness that can *only* be

1. Winston S. Churchill, *A Roving Commission* (New York: Charles Scribner's Sons, 1930), p. 13.

fulfilled in outer terms. Even our educational system places its final accent on the preparation of young men and women to meet the external trials and challenges of American life. . . . Those who are urging a return to the liberal arts have in mind the need for developing inner evaluations and for discovering how to achieve happiness in terms of them. But they are battling against heavy odds. Young people have been taught at home, and by all forms of communication and entertainment with which they come in contact, to externalize their values; hence, when choosing their college courses, they concentrate on that which will enable them to do this, whether it be "journalism," "home engineering," or "traffic safety." It seems to them no more than a kind of academic luxury to inquire into the inner meaning of Aeschylus or even to know who he was.[2]

St. Paul makes essentially the same point when, in writing to the Christians at Corinth, he observes that "the natural man receiveth not the things of the spirit of God for they are foolishness to him. Neither can he know them for they are spiritually discerned."[3]

What is true in the life of the spirit is true in the life of the mind. Regardless of the state of American culture, with its emphasis on things we can see and handle, education must continue to be concerned with the intangibles, the questions, the values, the deeper longings, and the unseen world of the

2. Russell Davenport, *The Dignity of Man* (New York: Harper and Row, 1965), pp. 108–109.

3. I Corinthians 2:14.

spirit. Education is preeminently concerned with man's inner life, man's development as a man, and what we mean by the dignity of man. Education goes off the track whenever it assumes, even subconsciously, that the great purpose of man's life is the happiness made possible by material and technological advance—with all its importance. If we remain insensitive to all but external values, the essential meaning of education will have escaped us.

If I were to choose a single analogy to help us understand the meaning, nature, and value of education I would direct our attention to mountain climbing. In a foreword to a book by Hugh Ruttledge entitled *Attack on Everest*, Sir Francis Younghusband remarks:

> to climb the highest mountain is an idea which makes immediate appeal. Those who would presume to pit themselves against the highest mountain in the world must be not only at the top of their physical development and be possessed of the highest mountaineering skill, but more important still, be animated by an invincible spirit, a spirit firm and tenacious and ambitious enough to drive on the body to its seemingly last extremity, yet selfless enough to throw away all hope of the prize in order to stand by a comrade or give place to another if through him the goal might more surely be achieved.
>
> So gradually there emerged the figure of Everest as a symbol of the loftiest spiritual height of man's imagination.[4]

4. Hugh Ruttledge, *Attack on Everest* (New York: Robert M. McBride and Co., 1935), pp. xvii–xix.

Some years before he lost his life on the northeast ridge of Mount Everest, in 1924, George Leigh Mallory was asked why the climbing of Mount Everest was such a challenge to him. He answered simply, "because it is there."[5]

This may not satisfy the cynic, but as we read the records of the many carefully planned expeditions that launched their assaults on Everest before its conquest in 1953, we begin to see what one writer called "a challenge high and impervious—waiting far above the earth for some man, finally to attain the summit—the top of the world."

We are creatures born for quest, shaped and fulfilled by quest. As Thomas F. Hornbein observes: "Of all resources the most crucial is Man's spirit. Not dulled, nor lulled, supine, secure, replete, does Man create; But out of stern challenge, in sharp excitement, with a burning joy; Man is the hunter still, though his quarry be a hope, a mystery, a dream."[6]

The challenge of mountain climbing throws a flood of light on the nature of man, and it is the nature of man as well as the nature of reality that is the concern of education. Lucien Devies expresses it this way: "The heights only give us what we ourselves bring to them. Climbing is a means of self-expression. Its justification lies in the men it develops, its heroes and its saints. Man overcomes himself, affirms himself and realizes himself in the struggle toward the summit, toward the absolute—then we know with absolute certainty that there is

5. Sir John Hunt, *The Conquest of Everest* (New York: E. P. Dutton, 1954), p. 8.

6. Thomas F. Hornbein, *Everest: The West Ridge* (London: Allen and Unwin, 1966).

something indestructible in us, against which nothing shall prevail."[7]

Or again Maurice Herzog tells us:

In overstepping our limitations, in touching the extreme boundaries of man's world, we have come to know something of its true splendor. In my worst moments of anguish, I seemed to discover the deep significance of existence, of which till then I had been unaware. I saw that it was better to be true than to be strong. The marks of the ordeal are apparent on my body. I was saved and I had won my freedom. This freedom, which I shall never lose, has given me the assurance and serenity of a man who has fulfilled himself. It has given me the rare joy of loving that which I used to despise—A new and splendid life has opened out before me.[8]

And, the last sentence of the book is the simple comment: "There are other Annapurnas in the life of men."[9]

We need not argue that education is as difficult as the climbing of Annapurna or Mount Everest. We can say, however, that the pursuit of knowledge is one of continuous and rigorous challenge and that it takes the same courage, the same concentration, and the same all-out effort to make a successful response to this challenge.

One of the recurring themes of Arnold Toynbee's *A*

7. Maurice Herzog, *Annapurna* (London: Jonathan Cape, 1952), p. 15.

8. Ibid., p. 12.

9. Ibid., p. 287.

Study of History is that the working of challenge and response explains not only the genesis of growth of a successful civilization, but also its breakdown and disintegration. Again and again he describes the successful response to the challenge of harsh and unfriendly climates, rocky and thin soil, and limited resources. Over and over we are told of cultural achievements that were due to the spur of adversity. It appears to be the lesson of history that man's finest response comes not from a life of ease but from one of struggle against heavy odds. As Cyrus observed: "Soft countries give birth to soft men."[10]

Hardship and sacrifice have their bright side as well as their dark. When the path has been made too easy, we cease to grow. In a study of old people Dr. Martin Gumpert reports in the New York *Times* that "A paradise where even the trees are good to eat, where the weather man has nothing to do because one perfect day follows another, where there are no worries, where strife and competition are unknown is no place for an animal or human population that wants to survive."

Two other scientists, Dr. Spencer and Dr. M. B. Melroy, reached a similar conclusion from a study with paramecium, a one-celled organism that reproduces itself year after year by multiplication. Drs. Spencer and Melroy created a paradise for paramecia. The temperature was right, the food was right, everything was right in that microscopic world. The pampered colony dies out much earlier than did control colonies that had to adapt themselves to environmental changes.

Jerome S. Bruner refers to the experiments at McGill

10. George Rawlinson, trans., *The History of Herodotus* (New York: D. Appleton, 1861–66), p. 394.

which demonstrate that "alertness depends on a constant regimen of dealing with environmental diversity." He points out that "the early challenges of problems to be mastered, of stresses to be overcome, are the preconditions of attaining some measure of our full potentiality as human beings. The child is father to the man . . . to make up for a bland impoverishment of experience early in life may be too great an obstacle for most organisms. Indeed, recent work indicates that for at least one species, the utilitarian rat, too much gray homogeneity in infancy may produce chemical changes in the brain that seem to be associated with dullness."[11]

There is nothing we can do about gray homogeneity in our infancy. Nor can we do anything about overprotection in the past. We can do something, however, about challenges and opportunities to grow and to learn for the rest of our lives.

Aristotle tells us that the function of man is an "activity of soul in accordance with reason, or not independently of reason."[12] It is the exercise of reason that distinguishes the educated person.

In the development of this noblest human power it is reassuring to know that the mountain is there. There are innumerable mountain ranges in the world of learning. There are those of art and music, of poetry and drama, of history and philosophy, of engineering and science, and many, many others. The majesty of our cultural heritage, the record of our aspiration and achievement, the greatest and best that has been

11. Jerome S. Bruner, *On Knowing—Essays for the Left Hand* (Cambridge, Mass.: Harvard University Press, 1962), p. 7.

12. Aristotle, *Nicomachean Ethics*, translated by J. E. C. Welldon (London: Macmillan, 1923), p. 16.

written and thought and lived await our acquaintance and our exploration. Yes, the mountain is there and it is a source of inspiration and challenge.

What then is education? It is what happens when men and mountains meet.

4

Jason and the Golden Fleece

O NE OF THE GREAT ADVENTURE STORIES of all time is the tale of Jason and his search for the Golden Fleece. Jason was a gifted young man who was educated by the Centaur, Chiron. When he reached manhood he went to Iolcus to claim the kingdom which his Uncle Pelias had stolen some twenty years before from his father, Aeson. To win the kingdom, however, he is commanded by crafty King Pelias to fetch the Fleece of the Golden Sheep. This was the golden coat of the sheep that had saved Phrixus and was now guarded by a dragon in the grove of Ares in Colchis. Jason calls together the noblest heroes in Greece—Orpheus, Castor, Pollux, Zetes, Theseus, and Heracles—to take part in the expedition. He then sets off in the *Argo*, a sturdy vessel of fifty oars that he and his friends build from the never-rotting pine from Mount Pelion.

We may not remember all the adventures of the voyage, for across the centuries men have added to the original account until it now has many versions and is a compendium of separate adventures that challenge memory and belief. Still, there are high peaks jutting through this cloud of myths; the visit to the island of Lemnos, peopled only by women who put to death all men, including their husbands, sons, and brothers; the encounter with Phineus, King of Salymydessus, who tells them what their course should be after they free him from the Harpies, who have been poisoning his food; their successful passage of the Symplegades—two gigantic moving rocks which close together and crush whatever ventures between them (they succeed by releasing a bird which flies between the rocks, losing a few of her tail feathers, and as the rocks are opening again the *Argo* dashes through); the battle with the man-eating Stymphalian birds of the islands of Aretias whose feathers are sharp as arrows; the journey by Mount Caucasus where they hear the groans of Prometheus chained to a rock with a vulture feasting upon his liver; and at the last the arrival of the Argonauts at the river Phasis. Sailing up the stream, they come upon the palace of Aeëtes, King of Colchis, possessor of the Golden Fleece. Jason is told that he must yoke fire-snorting bulls with hooves of brass, plough the field of Ares, then sow the land with dragon's teeth from which armed men spring. Undaunted, Jason performs these feats, then snatches the Fleece from the tree as the dragon stands docilely by, soothed by a tranquilizing potion given him by Medea, that mistress of magic and evil with such a gift for trouble. After a wild and dangerous voyage, Jason, taking Medea with him, arrives home safely and bears the Fleece victoriously to his uncle, King Pelias.

It is the lure of adventure and the quest of the difficult that give this story its ageless appeal. Man responds to the challenge of the difficult. The life of each of us, no matter how prosaic or uncomplicated on the surface, contains the thread of a continuing struggle toward an ultimate and transcending personal goal. Each has a special star toward which he steers. Each has his own private and special ambitions which can be achieved only by effort, struggle, and toil.

What is that we seek? What is the Golden Fleece we desire? Some of us are confident that we know. We have been influenced by the values, the achievements, and the hopes of our loved ones and friends. We have taken stock of our unique strengths and weaknesses, our interests and aptitudes, and have chosen our education and vocational goals. We should be prepared, however, for some surprises.

Much of what Jason experienced could not have been predicted. To a degree this is also true in the adventure of learning. The unpredictable happens, and when it does we must revise our plans and perhaps alter our course. Life goals change as we are challenged by new interests, experiences, and perspectives. If we should be caught by the magic of poetry when we thought we were headed for medicine, or we respond to the enchantment of music when our chief interest has been chemistry, this should not be totally unexpected. It is a normal experience. Indeed it is reassuring evidence that the leaven of learning is at work.

To wish that we could be both an actress and a psychiatrist, both an architect and a mathematician, both a scientist and a lawyer, both a businessman and a scholar is not a bad sign. More than one field should be attractive. What is disturbing is the man or woman who hears the beat of no drums and is unresponsive both to those at a distance and those near at hand.

The world of knowledge is one of endless wonder, fascination, and joy. Much of it is useful in the marketplace. It increases our influence and power. It frequently is a key to our advancement. It may even have its value in dollars. Fundamentally, however, education is not to be reverenced for its vocational contribution but for what it contributes to the living of life, not what it does for material affluence but what it makes possible in wealth of mind. Learning feeds our finest human hungers, meets our deepest needs, changes our interests, reshapes our values and ideals.

There must be commitment to the adventure of learning. As W. H. H. Murray reminds us:

Until one is committed there is hesitancy, the chance to draw back, always ineffectiveness. Concerning all acts of initiative (and creation), there is one elementary truth, the ignorance of which kills countless ideas and splendid plans: that the moment one definitely commits oneself, then Providence moves too. All sorts of things occur to help one that would never otherwise have occurred. A whole stream of events issues from the decision, raising in one's favour all manner of unforeseen incidents and meetings and material assistance which no man could have dreamt would have come his way.

I believe every soul has such moments of conviction and resolution,—moments when more by far than we can see depends upon how we act; when our own happiness and the happiness of others hang poised on the decision of a moment. It takes but an instant and a single revolution of the wheel to turn the ship, but by that movement it is decided whether she shall anchor on this side of the globe or on that. It takes but an instant for the mind to act, yet in the passing of a thought it is often settled what will be the direction and issue of a life.[1]

1. William H. H. Murray, *Music-Hall Sermons* (Boston: Fields, Osgood and Co., 1870), p. 9.

We need not press too far the resemblances between the exploits and ordeals of Jason and those we may have in our pursuit of learning. Both, however, are adventures. Because they are it may not be inappropriate to note that Jason demanded discipline as well as commitment. Commitment does not take us far without sacrifice and self-denial. We must learn to say "no" to ourselves as well as to our fellows. Indulgence does not build strength. Yielding to impulse and whim makes neither for stability nor joy. Having our own way does not help us to achieve maturity. The key to happiness, character, and learning is not freedom to do as we please, but commitment and self-control.

Another thing we need to learn is that excellence takes time. In *The Idea of History*, R. G. Collingwood notes that, "Just as Aristotle argued that a man cannot be happy in an instant, but that the possession of happiness takes a lifetime, so Mr. Whitehead argues that an atom of hydrogen takes time—the time necessary for establishing the peculiar rhythm of movements which distinguishes it from other atoms—so there is no such thing as 'nature at an instant.' "[2]

There is, of course, no such thing as education in an instant. It is a long, slow process. There are no short cuts. There is no substitute for hard work, dedication, practice, patient endurance. We hardly need to be told this if our goal is to be a pianist or a member of an Olympic team. What is so obvious in the search for excellence in music or sport applies with equal force in the field of learning.

In *The Education of Henry Adams*, Adams reports that in his seven years as a teacher, "The number of students

2. R. G. Collingwood, *The Idea of History* (Oxford: At the University Press, 1946), p. 212.

whose minds were of an order above the average was . . .
barely one in ten. The rest could not be much stimulated by
any inducements a teacher could suggest. All were respectable
and . . . Adams never had cause to complain of one; but nine
minds in ten take polish passively, like a hard surface; only
the tenth sensibly reacts."[3]

Far too many "take polish passively, like a hard surface." Since this will always be true, what we look for is someone, who in those wonderful words of Emerson, "shall make us
do what we can."[4] Most of us need this kind of help. It may
be an inspiring teacher, or a fellow student, or a friend. We
can do more than we think. As a rule our sights are much too
low. To do what we can, what we really can, to become all
that is possible, to develop our powers to their highest levels—
this is to find the meaning of human life. This is what the
quest is about.

It may be unfair to Jason and his heroic band, but in
the almost endless recital of their adventures, I find myself
asking the irreverent question: "Were all the adventures necessary?" The Argonauts were not angels. They were not models
of uprightness. They took some unnecessary detours. They
lost a lot of time they did not need to lose. And in the course
of their travels they sometimes forgot why they were there.

In the pursuit of learning we may have a like experience. We should remind ourselves from time to time to re-
examine our goals; and then move toward them.

3. *The Education of Henry Adams: An Autobiography* (Boston:
Houghton Mifflin, 1918), p. 302.

4. Our chief want in life is somebody who shall make us do what
we can—Ralph Waldo Emerson, *Conduct of Life* (Boston: Houghton
Mifflin, 1904), Vol. XVI, p. 272.

If in climbing a mountain toward a star we become too absorbed in the problem of climbing, we may forget which star is guiding us. If we move only for the sake of movement we will reach no destination.

We need to turn our back on competing interests and attractions, stop our ears, and shut out everything except the task to be done. To concentrate is to give all our attention. It is the extra effort of body and mind that makes such a world of difference. We should learn this early. We say to the beginner in tennis, "Keep your eye on the ball." To the stars at Wimbledon and Forest Hills we say, "Forget the crowd, forget the bad call, forget the error you just made, concentrate on winning the next point."

The Golden Fleece brought back by Jason was a treasure beyond price. It was worth all the sacrifice of time and effort. Apart from its own value it won for Jason the kingdom he so ardently desired. Our quest is different. We are concerned about something less tangible—the challenge of the beautiful, the true, the good; the inspiration of the best; a disciplined mind and a disciplined life; a new quality of manhood and womanhood. This also is a treasure, and one of far greater value than Jason's Fleece of Gold. It, too, is worth all the effort and all the cost. While in a literal sense it may not win a kingdom, it does give to those who seek it regal stature.

5

The Three R's

Alice was not sure that she was hearing what was said. The words sounded familiar, but they left her confused. Sometimes things are not what they seem to be. "We had the best of educations," said the Mock Turtle. . . . "I only took the regular course." "What was that?" inquired Alice. "Reeling and Writhing, of course, to begin with," the Mock Turtle replied, "and then the different branches of Arithmetic—Ambition, Distraction, Uglification, and Derision."[1]

We are confused too. We are troubled about the quality of education in America. In our case, it is the real world that confuses us, not a world of fantasy. Are the courts saying that the most important thing about American education is Riding? Are they telling us that Riding is one of the Three R's? Does sitting in a moving vehicle insure excellence in education? What is the mission of the schools? Is it education or

1. Lewis Carroll, *Alice's Adventures in Wonderland and Through the Looking Glass* (Philadelphia: John C. Winston, 1923), pp. 111–12.

something else? Like Alice, we hear the voice of the Mock Turtle, and we have our doubts.

No nation has had such a deep interest in education. None has spent so much for classroom buildings, laboratories, libraries, auditoria, gymnasia, swimming pools, tennis courts, and playing fields. None has spent so much for the training of its teachers, or has paid them so well. None has had such equipment and textbooks. Yet the evidence is overwhelming that there has been a decline in the quality of education in many parts of the nation, and particularly in the basic skills of reading, writing, speaking, and arithmetic.

To be sure, there are bright spots. In the field of organized team sports we have a new world. In the sciences we also have a very different world. We introduce students to science and technology at a much earlier age and they graduate from high school with a vastly wider knowledge of the basic sciences. Again, our brightest young people continue to amaze us. They are clearly very superior.

This, however, does not lessen our embarrassment as we see the deterioration of academic standards at all levels of American education. Through the introduction of more and more elective subjects the curriculum has been diluted. Traditional disciplines have been neglected or abandoned. The Three R's are a disaster area. It is in the basic areas like spelling, writing, reading, and arithmetic that the failure of our schools is greatest. We know about nuclear fission but we cannot spell it. We have learned how to use computers, but without them do not ask us to add, subtract, multiply, or divide. We are at home in the new world of television, radios, and stereophonic sound, but we no longer read.

Each year the College Entrance Examination Board

reports lower scores in the Verbal and in the Mathematical Tests. The examinations are not more difficult. Indeed they are easier. In our larger cities we are losing ground steadily in the reading skills of students. Remedial reading is given in the high schools in the hope that a junior high school reading level can be achieved before the students go on to college. The State of Arizona announces that it will try to raise the reading level of its high school students to that of the ninth grade. The State of New York has also announced the adoption of the same goal. Yet we have never had better textbooks or such an army of librarians and reading specialists. We have also had the wonders of educational television, with its "Sesame Street."

Our failure is equally notable in the speaking and writing of English. To write a paragraph with words correctly spelled and the sentences free from grammatical error is beyond the ability of many of us, including a goodly number of college students.

Recently a distinguished business executive addressed a group of faculty members and students in a well-regarded community college. In the discussion that followed one of the students said, "Y' know, y'know, I'd like to have a swell job as you, man. Y'know, y'know, I wanna be, y'know what I mean, a President too, y'know. Wadda ya have to do, y'know, to get your job?" The business executive waited for a minute and then replied quietly, "First, you learn to speak English."

The comment of Henry Higgins to Liza Doolittle, the flower girl, in Shaw's *Pygmalion* may be dramatic hyperbole, but it says it all: "A woman who utters such depressing and disgusting sounds has no right to be anywhere—no right to live. Remember that you are a human being with a soul and the divine gift of articulate speech: that your native language is the language of Shakespeare and Milton and the Bible; and don't sit there crooning like a bilious pigeon."

And then he addressed the others, "You see this creature with her curbstone English: the English that will keep her in the gutter to the end of her days. Well sir, in three months I could pass that girl off as a dutchess at an ambassador's garden party."[2]

We may not have a Henry Higgins to help us, and we may not care about ambassadors' garden parties. Nevertheless, correct speech should be our first objective. The purchase of a good dictionary should be followed by its almost daily use. Whenever there is a question about the spelling or the meaning of a word we should look it up. And we do not do it the next day; we do it on the spot. The habit of using the dictionary will help not only our spelling, but our pronunciation and our use of words. Let us learn the exact meaning of the word. If we look up a verb let us find out about its noun, adjective, and adverb. Note the derivation of the word and its original meaning in Greek, Latin, Hebrew, or what.

Most of us are unduly sensitive about the correction of our errors. We should encourage our friends to correct us. I well remember an afternoon long ago in my fraternity house at Syracuse when Professor Raymond F. Piper of the Philosophy department called on me. The visit was unexpected. I had been studying in my room and when summoned to the living room on the first floor I was wearing neither a coat nor a tie. In the 1920s this was of some importance. I was embarrassed and I apologized for my appearance. "Think nothing

2. George Bernard Shaw, *Androcles and the Lion, Overruled, Pygmalion* (London: Constable, 1916), Act I, pp. 114–15.

of it," said Professor Piper. "I have come with a list of words you mispronounce. I did not want to speak about this in the presence of other students. I don't know what you will become in the years after you leave the university, but you will find it useful to speak correctly."

What a wonderful thing for a teacher to do! I was touched and could have hugged him with gratitude. Would that each of us had a Professor Piper to help us!

For many years the catalogue of Hamilton College carried this statement: "Hamilton believes that every educated man should be able to stand upon his feet before a group and express himself clearly. Every Hamilton student is required to include four years of public speaking in his curriculum."[2] Four years of public speaking is no longer a requirement for graduation at Hamilton. Not too long ago, I met a senior at Hamilton who defended the dropping of the requirement. "It was no longer relevant," he said, "What we have now is a fabulous course in Ecology."[3]

Ecology is important too, and particularly the conservation of our uniquely human resources. The mastery of the basic tools of learning is, however, always relevant. This is one objective that should not change.

Jacques Barzun, in his *Teacher in America*, reminds us that

> In the lower schools, one has, or used to have the excellent practice of daily recitation. The pupil stands up and speaks before the class. Excess of it is dull, but used

3. Quoted in Joseph G. Brin, *Speech and Human Relations* (Boston: Bruce Humphries, 1946), p. 6.

in moderation it is the proper start of a training which should end with frequent oral examinations and public speaking in college. Is it not evident that every doctor, lawyer, teacher, engineer, architect, business executive, should be able to think on his feet and talk about his subject? I should except only dentists, whose crowning merit is golden silence.[4]

It probably serves no useful purpose to lament the decline of debate and public speaking in schools and colleges. We shall have to teach ourselves to speak. We can do so if we try. The principles of public speaking are relatively simple. Once mastered what we need is practice.

First of all we should have good posture. Let us stand as tall as we can, erect without being stiff. We must not fidget. We keep our hands naturally at our sides. We do not put them in our pockets. We do not touch our nose or pull our ears. We keep the weight of our body on the balls of our feet rather than on the heels. We do not rock from heel to toe. We are not glued to one spot, but we do not pace back and forth. We do not overdo the use of gestures, particularly at first. We look at our audience. We single out two or three of them and speak directly to them. We avoid mumbling. We do not swallow our words. We open our mouth. We speak clearly. We put warmth in our voice. (Nothing is so bad as a listless voice.) We raise our voice. It is better to speak too loudly than not to be heard. We use emphasis, inflection, color, variety of tone, friendliness, and life. Our voice is a wind instrument. We must learn to play it.

4. Jacques Barzun, *Teacher in America* (New York: Doubleday Anchor, 1959), pp. 189–90.

We avoid the use of "uh" and "er." To err is human, but in public speaking it is a sure way to distract and irritate our audience.

We should try to be natural, simple, sincere, and confident. We choose our words carefully. We avoid long words if there are shorter words with the same meaning. We avoid the use of too many technical terms or professional jargon. We use as few clichés as we can. We avoid verbosity and circumlocution. We try to be brief and clear.

For audiences not interested in our subject we use our strongest argument first. For audiences that are interested we use our best argument last.

We do not worry about stage fright. A little nervousness may be a good thing. We all speak better when we are fully alert. If we become self-conscious we might begin thinking about how we will put our audience at ease. Thinking about them will take our mind off our own nervousness.

We have never had one, but you might buy a tape recorder and use it to hear yourself. You may be surprised, and perhaps disappointed, but there is no reason to get discouraged! You will improve steadily with practice! A good way to practice is to read aloud.

If learning to speak correctly and effectively is one of our goals, learning to write is another. We learn to write by writing. It is as simple as that. It is like walking. A baby stands and falls. She stands and falls again. The failures seem endless, but she is not afraid to fail. Eventually she stands without falling. When she takes a step she may fall again, but this does not discourage her. Falling—temporary failure—is the price she pays. She pays it over and over until she learns to walk.

In writing we must be prepared to fail. Our first efforts are hopeless, or so it seems. We cannot write a single sentence that is simple and clear. We have a mental block about putting words on paper. They will not come. We sit there for minutes at a time. We become more and more nervous and frustrated. The game seems hardly worth the candle.

The only advice one can give is to begin writing. We will not like what we have written, so we begin again, and again. When we have our first page we read it silently, and then aloud. We look at each sentence. We rewrite each sentence. We substitute verbs and nouns. We change or strike out the adjectives. We go to the dictionary for prefixes, suffixes, synonyms, and antonyms. We correct the grammatical errors. We eliminate the word *got* from the sentence: "My wife has got brown eyes." We look carefully at our use of prepositions. We eliminate double negatives. We make sentences of non-sentences by inserting a subject and a verb. We strike out all unnecessary words (we call this the use of Ockham's Razor.)

> The written word
> Should be as clean as a bone,
> Clear as light,
> Firm as a stone.
> Two words are not
> As good as one.[5]

5. Helen R. Hull, ed., *The Writer's Book* (New York: Harper and Brothers, 1950), p. 275. See also William Strunk, Jr.—E. B. White, *Elements of Style*, 2nd ed. (New York: Macmillan, 1972), a most useful book.

The poet Yeats said it this way, in "Adam's Curse":

> I said a line will take us
> hours may be,
> Yet if it does not seem a
> moment's thought,
> The stitching and unstitching has been
> for naught.[6]

Jonathan Swift used to read what he had written to his charwoman. If she understood and gave her approval Swift knew he had achieved clarity and simplicity.

Churchill at the age of thirteen was at the bottom of the bottom form at Harrow. He stayed there for more than a year. This, however, had two advantages: he gave his undivided attention to the study of English and he had a superb teacher. As he tells the story,

> By being so long in the lowest form, I gained an immense advantage over the cleverer boys. They all went on to learn Latin and Greek and splendid things like that. But I was taught English. We were considered such dunces that we could learn only English. Mr. Somervell— a most delightful man, to whom my debt is great—was charged with the duty of teaching the stupidest boys the most disregarded thing: namely, to write mere English. He knew how to do it. He taught it as no one else has ever taught it. Not only did we learn English parsing thoroughly, but we also practised continually English

6. William Butler Yeats, *Selected Poems* (New York: Macmillan, 1921), p. 158.

analysis. Mr. Somervell had a system of his own. He took a fairly long sentence and broke it up into its component parts by means of black, red, blue, and green inks. Subject, verb, object; Relative Clauses, Conditional Clauses, Conjunctive and Disjunctive Clauses! Each had its colour and its bracket. It was a kind of drill. We did it almost daily. As I remained in the Third Fourth . . . three times as long as anyone else, I had three times as much of it. I learned it thoroughly. Thus I got into my bones the essential structure of the ordinary British sentence—which is a noble thing. And when in after years my school fellows who had won prizes and distinctions for writing such beautiful Latin poetry and pithy Greek epigrams had to come down again to common English, to earn their living or make their way, I did not feel myself at any disadvantage. Naturally I am biased in favor of boys learning English; I would make them all learn English: and then I would let the clever ones learn Latin as an honour, and Greek as a treat. But the only thing I would whip them for is not knowing English. I would whip them hard for that.[7]

I shall say nothing about arithmetic, but because of the importance of reading and the decline in reading skills, let us address ourselves briefly to the first of the Three R's.

Most of us approach the question of reading from the point of view of speed. We are anxious to increase the rate of speed at which we read. For many of us the first problem is to cure ourselves of the habit of moving our lips as we read. To read at a faster rate than we speak we learn to read phrases

7. Winston S. Churchill, *A Roving Commission* (New York: Charles Scribner's Sons, 1930), pp. 166–67.

instead of separate words. We should read a line with as few eye movements as possible.

The first requirement is to want to increase our reading speed. Our degree of concentration will depend on our motivation. To keep ourselves alert, we ask questions and quiz ourselves. We use a watch to drill ourselves in faster reading. We learn to skip and skim and look for ideas. We build our word power. We pace ourselves.

When we are reading for information we can save time by pre-reading. By this we mean turning first to the title page, then to the table of contents, and then to the foreword or preface, and finally to the index. This does not apply to books of poetry, drama, or fiction. For nonfiction, however, the title page may disclose a subtitle and it may tell us something about the author. The table of contents will help to give a general outline of the book. The preface, and particularly the opening and closing paragraphs, will throw light on the author's point of view and his special interest and purpose. The index will tell us where to find the material of greatest interest to us.

For anyone who reads widely reading speed does not remain a problem. We adjust our speed to the degree of difficulty of our reading materials. We read a novel or detective story quickly, a book on philosophy or mathematics slowly, and a book on economics, history, or political science at moderate speed.

In much of our reading speed is meaningless. Frequently we immerse ourselves in the ideas, images, or the narrative of the author. We enter the timeless world of reflection where we want an answer to our questions. We may carry on a dialogue with the writer. We pause to make notes. If it is a book that belongs to us, and one we may read again, we may underline passages and make marginal notes. We are reading to remember, to think about the meaning of what we have been reading, and to reflect, debate, agree, or admire.

Our first goal in reading is to understand what we are reading. The first test is to comprehend fully so that we can report accurately. This requires close attention. We frequently do not give our full attention to the people who speak to us, and we are equally guilty when we read. To read carefully, to understand clearly, and to report accurately are no mean achievements. Good reporting is rare, and the reason for its rarity is inattention in listening and reading.

Reading comprehension may be our first goal, but it is not our only one. An even more important goal is to read thoughtfully and critically. We must bring to what we are reading an alert, active, questioning mind. Reading is an exercise in thought. It involves analysis and evaluation. It is the use of logic as well as attention and memory. It is more than comprehension and storage for instant retrieval. Reading is the critical examination of thesis, antithesis, and synthesis, the whole process of thought.

We are all familiar with the comment that lectures can be given by teachers and repeated by students without passing through the mind of either. Frequently we can give a fairly full report of what we have heard from someone on television or read in a book or magazine without asking a single question as to its slant or degree of truth.

One of the problems in the early Middle Ages was the reverence for anything one found written in a manuscript. When books were rare whatever was written was presumed to be true. With our flood of books and paperbacks there is no excuse for being so trusting and respectful. Yet it is still true that the comments of our television pundits and the words we read in print carry more authority than they should. Most of us absorb what we read quite uncritically.

I was reminded of this in my senior year as an undergraduate. I had enrolled in a course in "The Philosophy of Religion" given by Professor George A. Wilson, the chairman of the Philosophy Department. The textbook was by George Galloway. It was an excellent book and I read it several times. On the final examination I was sure I had done well. Professor Wilson was a remarkable teacher. He taught his students to think for themselves. The comment he wrote on my examination paper was: "Excellent on Galloway. What about Tolley?" The feedback so many teachers want was not enough for Professor Wilson. It should not be enough for any of us. Let us examine critically everything we hear and everything we read.

If we are serious about improving the quality of American education we should begin by improving instruction in the Three R's. That instruction is the responsibility of all teachers—chemists, biologists, mathematicians, economists, philosophers, and all the others. It is too important to be left only to the teacher of speech and English composition.

In becoming all we can be, we also begin with the Three R's. By practice and by use we increase our mastery of these basic skills. We may not read widely or deeply enough. We may not speak or write as well as we should like. If however, we work at it we shall go much further than we think we can at the beginning of the journey.

6

Eyes to See

ON OF MAN, the prophet Ezekiel reminds us, "Thou dwell-est in the midst of a rebellious house, which have eyes to see and see not; they have ears to hear, and hear not."[1]

Not the easiest or least important problem, whether it be in education or religion, is to teach people to see and to hear. Stated negatively education is the removal of handicaps. It is the release from what limits and confines. It is the escape from crippling influences and stunted growth. Lack of education is a deafness and a blindness. Without development the mind does not function. We then have eyes to see and see not, ears to hear and hear not.

Stated positively education teaches us how to see and how to hear, how to speak and how to think, how to read, how to express ourselves in written form and how to master the use of numbers. As our learning grows and our experience deepens we become more perceptive, we listen for sounds and meanings not previously heard, we are more skilled in speech, more accurate in observation and analysis, more adept in

1. Ezekiel 12:2.

handling general and abstract ideas, more critical of error in logic and intellectual inquiry, and more familiar with the fantastic march of modern science and other fields of knowledge. The range of our intellectual interests is increased. As the mind finds new interests, the growth is three-dimensional, with surprising height and breadth and depth.

In this process of growth we come to see books as the bread of the intellect. The mind must be fed and books must be a large part of the diet. Moreover, the quality and kind of books it feeds upon makes a critical difference. The place of books, their importance, choice, and use, is central in the pursuit of learning. By them the individual man consults the universal man. By them a solitary, isolated single mind comes to grips with the genius of the human race.

At no level is education a spectator sport. It is only for players, and it must be played hard. Education demands the most rigorous training and self-discipline. It requires all our effort and devotion. Moreover, it is the joining of experience and thought, art and science, imagination and reason, belief and action.

In the joining of these different approaches to truth a large part of education is an exercise in seeing. The reader who looks up the word *see* in Roget's *Thesaurus* is referred to three other words: *Attention, Knowledge,* and *Vision.* Surely this is a trilogy of learning. Seeing includes the meaning of all three. It is not to be confused with attention, knowledge, and vision disjoined and isolated from each other.

We are all familiar with the facile mind that is essentially a photographic memory. A quick grasp of the printed page, a flypaper retention of knowledge for at least a brief period, and a letter-perfect reproduction of the textbook and the instructor's lectures give this type of student a tremendous advantage over his fellows. Seeing, however, is something far beyond memory and feedback. It goes beyond even the amazing feats of mechanical computers. Seeing calls for insights, understandings, and satisfactions neither the parrot nor the computer can have. Nonetheless, it embraces everything both can do.

Seeing involves judgment as well as memory. "A man with a good memory but no judgment," says Kant, "is merely a walking dictionary. . . . Intelligence divorced from judgment produces nothing but foolishness. Understanding is the knowledge of the general. Judgment is the application of the general to the particular. Reason is the power of understanding the connection between the general and the particular."[2] Yes, seeing is understanding, judgment, and reason.

Seeing involves both that which can be photographed and measured and that which cannot. Increasingly we must be concerned with science and mathematics. We do not understand the possibilities of the future without a great deal more sophistication in science and mathematics than would have been thought necessary even a decade ago. But in thinking about what our education should eventually provide, even science and mathematics are only a part of the answer.

Seeing is many-sided. It embraces all of art, and particularly art in daily life, sensitivity to beauty as a constant source of pleasure and meaning. Stretching its literal meaning it includes all the senses, listening as well as looking, smelling, tasting, and feeling. It involves the body as well as the mind,

2. *Kant on Education*, translated by Abnetta Churton (Boston, Mass.: D. C. Heath, 1900), p. 71.

the sensuous images as well as those of the spirit. It has a special place for aesthetic appreciation.

Take for example the words of W. H. Hudson when he writes: "I feel when I am out of sight of living, growing grass and out of the sound of birds' voices and all rural sounds, that I am not properly alive." He goes on to say, "when I hear people say that they have not found the world and life so agreeable and interesting as to be in love with it, or that they look with equanimity to its end, I am apt to think that they have never been properly alive, nor seen with clear vision the world they think so meanly of or anything in it,— not even a blade of grass."[3]

Vision in the sense of aesthetic response needs vastly more attention. Our general blindness to beauty in nature is but illustrative of underdeveloped powers and appreciations in almost every aspect of life. We need the insight of imagination. And we need art as life and human experience.

If education is the process by which we learn to see, what else does seeing mean? Perhaps a single illustration in depth will suggest some answers. What do we see when a picture of the Chartres Cathedral is shown to us in a photograph or on the screen? How much more do we see when we are privileged to visit Chartres and walk in and around it, perhaps to stay there for the day—or see it many times, looking at it again and again? How much more do we see if we have an interesting and instructive guide? How much more do we see if we are familiar with the history of art, the history of religion, and the history of the cathedral itself?

3. William Henry Hudson, *Far Away and Long Ago* (New York: Limited Edition Club, 1943), p. 307.

Certainly what we see depends in part on how attentive, how sensitive, and how responsive we are. It may depend too on interest and motivation. Assuming these, it still depends on knowledge. What we see always depends on how much we know. Knowledge does not guarantee sight but it is perhaps the most important requirement.

To the thousands of tourists who come to see Chartres each day the cathedral is a masterpiece of art and architecture and a supreme achievement of religious devotion. Its magnificent design makes an almost overwhelming impression. As William Fleming remarks in his *Arts and Ideas*, "When the harmonious proportions of the west façade art are first observed everything seems as right as immutable truth."[4] Not until we have done some reading or have been instructed by a guide are we likely to see the evidence of improvisation in the moving of the triple portal and the lancet windows after the fire of 1194. (They were moved forward forty feet to be flush with the two towers for the spires.) Nor would we necessarily notice that in filling the central part of the façade the famous rose window is slightly off-center.

But even when we are adequately informed, what do we look for and what do we see? Is it primarily technical details such as the difference in the height of the spires (one of 350 feet, the other 377) or the remarkable equilibrium of weights and balances in the quadripartite cross vaulting of the apse, the pointed arches, shafts, colonettes, and clustered columns, the flying buttresses, pinnacles, and piers? Are we conscious of the art which draws the eye ir-

4. William Fleming, *Arts and Ideas*, 3rd ed. (New York: Holt, Rinehart and Winston, 1968), p. 190.

resistibly upward by steadily rising vertical lines, the rich symbolism in the profusion of sculpture (more than 2,000 carved figures between the west façade and the north and south porches of the transepts), the play of light making an ever-changing mosaic of warm colors, the rare blues of the older windows, the contrast in architectural styles between the spire built in 1180 so admired by specialists in art, and the slimmer, taller, and more elegant spire built more than three hundred years later (from 1507–13)?

Are we particularly intrigued by the stories in pictures in the stained glass windows, one of the early forms of comic books? They are pictures which recounted tales for people who could not read. They tell the stories of common people—bakers, furriers, wheelwrights and barrel-makers— as well as traditional religious figures and themes. Do we see it, as did Vincent of Beauvais in his *Speculum Majus,* through its carved figures, its iconography? If so, we can approach Chartres as a unique visual encyclopedia of medieval learning. It portrays and brings together all that the medieval world knew of nature, instruction, history, and morality. In the flora and fauna so exactly and comprehensively represented we see the mirror of nature.

In the personification of the Trivium (Grammar, Rhetoric, and Dialectic) and the Quadrivium (Geometry, Arithmetic, Astronomy, and Music) we see the curriculum of the cathedral school. They are the seven liberal arts which were the sum of learning for centuries. At Chartres there is a person and a figure for each of the seven. We meet Aristotle and the figure of Dialectic, Cicero and Rhetoric, Euclid and Geometry, Boethius and Arithmetic, Ptolemy and Astronomy, Donatus and Grammar, and Pythagoras and Music with her monochord, a psaltery, a three-stringed viol, and a three-chimed bell.[5]

And when we find our way to the north porch, which was built a century later, we learn that there are now universities as well as cathedral schools. So we see a figure representing Philosophy, again with Aristotle, who was regarded as the greatest of philosophers, and to our surprise, figures representing the two practical disciplines that had been excluded from the seven liberal arts: Architecture, represented by Archimedes, and Medicine with a figure of Hippocrates.

Because the mirror of learning must be complete we also see Apelles and a figure of Painting; Tubal-Cain and the Metal crafts; and Adam, Abel, and Cain in a group of figures representing Agriculture. Thus in one building the whole story of history is told. The iconography depicts the story of mankind from Adam and Eve to the Day of the Last Judgment, the story of Christ from his ancestors to his Resurrection and Ascension, the story of Mary, traced from man's creation to her coronation in Heaven, and on the south porch, the wonderful story of man's redemption through the Church and its saints, popes, abbots, and bishops, again to the final day of judgment.

There is also the great mirror of morality. We see the figures of vice and virtue, the foolish and the wise virgins, the damned and the saved, and the gargoyles and the devils fleeing before the saints and angels.

It is all there. It is an encyclopedia of ancient lore and

5. See Adolph Katzenellenbogen, *Twelfth Century Europe* and *The Foundation of Modern Society; The Representation of the Seven Liberal Arts* (Madison: University of Wisconsin Press, 1966), pp. 39–54. Cf. also *The School of Chartres* by Raymond Klibansky, and *The Iconography of The Seven Liberal Arts. Stained Glass*, XXVII, p. 3–17.

contemporary history; it tells us of prophecy and fact, the animals of fable and mythology and those of the real world, the place of tradesmen and prices, old wives' tales and the latest knowledge of the schools.

Again, we may approach Chartres not as an architectural model, a museum, or a visual encyclopedia of learning but as a place of worship; and we may see it only or primarily as such.

Or finally we may see it as a center of community life, see it in terms of its influence not on tourists but on the people who live in Chartres. We may view it in terms of earlier community life—the life of stonecutters, masons, carpenters, metal workers, nobles, and princes of which we get a vignette in that delightful letter of Abbot Haimon of Normandy to his brother monks in Tutbury, England. After a visit to Chartres the Abbot wrote:

> Who has ever heard tell, in times past, that powerful princes of the world, that men brought up in honor and wealth, that nobles, men and women, have bent their proud and haughty necks to the harness of carts, and that, like beasts of burden, they have dragged to the abode of Christ these waggons, loaded with wines, grains, oil, stone, wood, and all that is necessary for the wants of life, or for the construction of the church. . . .
>
> When they have reached the church, they arrange the wagons about it like a spiritual camp, and during the whole night they celebrate the watch by hymns and canticles. On each wagon they light tapers and lamps; they place there the infirm and sick, and bring them the precious relics of the Saints for their relief.[6]

6. Fleming, *Arts and Ideas*, p. 183.

The point of all this is that seeing is many things. It is seeing in depth. It is an attempt to see all there is to see.

We may take any one of a thousand illustrations from science, government, or other fields and the problem will be the same: to look beyond the obvious, to look hard and to see as much as possible. Whether one is dealing with a problem in mathematics, looking through a microscope in a laboratory or gazing at the heavens on a starlight night, it is always possible to see more than we have seen before.

In the seventh book of the *Republic*, Plato sums up the difficulty in problems of seeing and knowing in his famous "Allegory of the Cave." He describes a group of men living in an underground den since childhood, chained so that they cannot look toward the mouth of the cave where a blazing fire is set. Between them and this source of light there is a wall, along the top of which pass an endless parade of "vessels, and statues and figures of animals, made of wood and stone."

Plato compares the situation of these men with the conditions of our existence in the world. We are unable to view clearly and directly the objects and events which fill our lives. Like the captives of the cave, we can know ourselves and interpret our experience only imperfectly. Like these prisoners who see only the flickering shadows on the wall of the cave, we must grope and fumble for the truth.

Having described this setting, Plato speculates on what might happen if one of these men were to break loose from his chains and were compelled to turn ablaze with the light of the sun. Plato tells us:

> He will require to grow accustomed to the sight of the upper world. And first he will see the shadows best, next the reflections of men and other objects in the water, and

then the objects themselves; then he will gaze upon the light of the moon and the stars and the spangled heaven; and he will see the sky and the stars by night better than the sun or the light of the sun by day. Last of all he will be able to see the sun, and not mere reflections of him in the water, but he will see him as he is in his own proper place, and not in another, and he will contemplate his nature.[7]

Our culture is the culture of the cave. It is a world of shadows. The mission of the school and college is to help people out of their darkness and into light. Some carry their chains to the end of their lives. Others escape from their bonds and emerge into the blinding world of light, but are never able to see more than shadows and reflections of reality. Others come to see clearly an object or two, while some apprehend a vast range of reality. Only a handful are able to look into the sun.

But this is our goal. This is the lure of learning. The adventure of learning is to help us gaze at the spangled heavens, even at the sun of truth itself.

7. Plato, *The Republic*, Book VII, translated by Benjamin Jowett (New York: Charles Scribner's Sons, 1890), Vol. II., pp. 342–43.

7

Three Stages of Learning

D O WE NOT CREEP before we walk? Do we not walk before we run? Should we not run before we try to fly? Isaiah, however, was not wrong when he said, "They shall mount up with wings as eagles; they shall run and not be weary; and they shall walk and not faint."[1] He had the art of becoming in the right order. As children we have an insatiable curiosity about the world and everything in it. We are also filled with endless wonder. We have a great desire to catch up with our older brothers and sisters, to do what they do and to know what they know. In our curiosity and impatience, we experience the joy of countless new discoveries. Propelled by wonder and curiosity we mount up with wings as eagles.

If the first stage of learning is one of curiosity and wonder, the second is the development of habits of accuracy, exactness, and precision. From a stage of novelty, discovery, and romance we move to one of identification and classification. We train our memory, we study the anatomy of language. We master English grammar and composition. We learn

1. Isaiah 40:31.

our arithmetic, algebra, and geometry. This is the great period
of observation. It is also a time for the discovery of the
structure of words, sentences, ideas, and numbers. If we have
a good teacher we look for relationships between ideas. We
begin to see things in context. We look for connections and
fundamental ideas. We are learning to run and not be weary.

The third and final stage of learning is the search for
principles and the mastery of abstract thought. This is the
most difficult part of learning. When we are filled with curiosity and a sense of wonder we mount up with wings as eagles.
As we learn to observe things accurately, master the Three
R's, and begin to look for relationships between ideas, the
going gets rougher. The problem is to run and not be weary.
The hardest part, however, is to deal with ideas, discover general principles, and build a solid structure of connected knowledge. This is when we learn to walk and not faint.

In most of our schools and colleges there is a heavy
emphasis on facts, whether related or not. The lecture method
so widely used need not mean that only facts are important,
but with rare exceptions this is the case. Yet as Jacques Barzun
tells us:

> The only thing worth teaching anybody is a principle.
> Naturally principles involve facts and some facts must be
> learned "bare" because they do not rest on any principle.
> The capital of Alaska is Juneau and, so far as I know,
> that is all there is to it; but a European child ought not
> learn that Washington is the capital of the United States
> without fixing firmly in mind the relation between the
> city and the man who led his countrymen to freedom.
> That would be missing an association, which is the germ

of a principle. And just as a complex athletic feat is made possible by rapid and accurate coordination, so all valuable learning hangs together and *works* by associations which make sense.[2]

Whitehead describes the three stages of learning with particular insight:

The whole period of growth from infancy to manhood forms one grand cycle. The stage of romance stretches across the first dozen years of its life, its stage of precision comprises the whole school period of secondary education, and its stage of generalization is the period of entrance into manhood. For those whose formal education is prolonged beyond the school age, the University course or its equivalent is the great period of generalization. The spirit of generalization should dominate a University. The lectures should be addressed to those to whom details and procedure are familiar; that is to say, familiar at least in the sense of being so congruous to pre-existing training as to be easily acquirable. During the school period the student has been mentally bending over his desk; at the University level he should stand up and look around. For this reason it is fatal if the first year at the University be frittered away in going over the old work in the old spirit. At school the boy painfully rises from the particular toward glimpses at general ideas; at the University he should start from general ideas and study their application to concrete cases. A well-planned University course

2. Jacques Barzun, *Teacher in America* (New York: Mentor, 1959), p. 25.

is a study of the wide sweep of generality. I do not mean that it should be abstract in the sense of divorce from concrete fact, but that concrete fact should be studied as illustrating the scope of general ideas.

The really useful training yields a comprehension of a few general principles with a thorough grounding in the way they apply to a variety of concrete details. . . . The function of a University is to enable you to shed details in favour of principles. . . . I can put my point otherwise by saying that the idea of the University is not so much knowledge, as power. Its business is to convert the knowledge of a boy into the power of a man.[3]

In recent years we have been learning more and more about the intellectual development of children. It is clear that we have wasted many years of learning time because of the fear that students were not ready or the subject was too difficult. With the exception of the earliest stage of childhood the truth is that almost nothing is too difficult. Jerome S. Bruner says: "The foundation of any subject may be taught to anybody at any age in some form."[4]

The stage of generalization so well stated by Whitehead should not be delayed until students reach the university. We need an accent on structure and fundamental principles all through the school years. Attention to this will narrow the gap between elementary and advanced knowledge.

3. Alfred North Whitehead, *The Aims of Education* (New York: Mentor, 1953), pp. 37–39.

4. Jerome S. Bruner, *The Process of Education*, rev. ed. (Cambridge, Mass.: Harvard University Press, 1977), p. 12.

At all levels we should try to connect ideas and look for underlying principles. Bruner reminds us:

the curriculum of a subject should be determined by the most fundamental understanding that can be achieved of the underlying principles that give structure to that subject. Teaching specific topics of skills without making clear their context in the broader fundamental structure in a field of knowledge is uneconomical in several deep senses. In the first place, such teaching makes it exceedingly difficult for the student to generalize from what he has learned to what he will encounter later. In the second place, learning that has fallen short of a grasp of general principles has little reward in terms of intellectual excitement. The best way to create interest in a subject is to render it worth knowing, which means to make the knowledge gained usable in one's thinking beyond the situation in which the learning has occurred. Third, knowledge one has acquired without sufficient structure to tie it together in knowledge is likely to be forgotten. An unconnected set of facts has a pitiably short half-life in memory. Organizing facts in terms of principles and ideas from which they may be inferred is the only known way of reducing the quick rate of loss of human memory.[5]

Regardless of our age, the elements of wonder, exactness, and the relationships of ideas continue to be present in all our active learning. When we acquire a telescope and study the stars for the first time, the sense of wonder, discovery, and delight is the same whether we are twenty years old or

5. Ibid., pp. 31–32.

sixty. When we read Homer or Goethe there is the same sense of awe and excitement. The romance of learning does not lessen as we grow older. Indeed for many, having been long removed from the classroom with its surfeit of recitation and instruction, there is a rebirth of curiosity and wonder.

Foreign languages may be a bit more difficult to learn, particularly if we do not have a good ear for them. In other fields, however, we do not mind the discipline of exactness, definiteness, and independent power of analysis. To our great comfort, moreover, the third and most difficult stage of learning is well within our reach. Indeed we shall do better than when we were undergraduates. Working with ideas is a challenge which evokes immediate response.

Our primary problem may be that we are too easily discouraged. If we have been away from serious study we may find it more difficult than we had expected it to be. The veterans who returned to college after long years of war had this experience. All found a civilian classroom a very difficult world. They had to make a conscious effort to read and to study. The first weeks were not easy. If, however, they were able to cross the first threshold of discouragement, it was much easier from that point. And so it should be with us!

In tackling any new subject we are at a disadvantage until we are familiar with the vocabulary and have enough knowledge to recognize some general ideas. The mind is like a coat rack, and general ideas are like the hooks on the rack. Once we have enough hooks in place we can hang things on them. Our progress in a new field is slow until we have a foundation of facts that are connected and details that are in a structured pattern.

Henri Poincaré in his *Science and Method* speaks of

making combinations that "reveal to us unsuspected kinship between . . . facts long known, but wrongly believed to be strangers to one another."[6] Much of what we call scientific discovery is arranging the evidence in new ways and the fresh insights that come from the new arrangement.

We may not make any earth-shaking discoveries, but as we look for general principles and study the relation of ideas we shall see the regularities of previously unrecognized relationships and similarities between ideas. In addition to specific applications to tasks that are similar we shall use general ideas as a basis for recognizing other ideas that are related or similar. This is the heart of the learning process.

6. Quoted in Jerome Bruner, *On Knowing—Essays for the Left Hand* (Cambridge, Mass.: Harvard University Press, 1962), p. 19.

8

The Uncommon Life

W E HAVE BEEN TOLD for a long time that this is the age of the common man. Perhaps we need to remind ourselves that the age of the common man was made possible by uncommon men. The age of the common man can be lifted out of cheapness and conformity only by uncommon men. Whatever our role in life we can all aspire to be uncommon in the quality of our minds, our character, and our service.

What expectations do we have a right to hold as the consequences of education? What image of outcomes ought we to envision? First, education should lead to emotional maturity. In its most comprehensive sense education represents man's permanent struggle for maturity. It is the process by which he grows up into freedom, and only the mature can be free.

Walter Lippman in his *Preface to Morals* says:

We grow older, but it is by no means certain that we grow up. The human character is a complicated thing, and its elements do not necessarily march in step. It is possible to be a sage in some things and a child in others, to be at once precocious and retarded, to be shrewd and foolish, serene and irritable. For some parts of our personalities may well be more mature than others, not infrequently we participate in the enterprise of an adult with the mood and manners of a child.

The successful passage into maturity depends, therefore, on a breaking up and reconstruction of those habits which were appropriate only to our earliest experience.

In a certain larger sense, this is the essence of education. For unless a man has acquired the character of an adult, he is a lost soul no matter how good his technical equipment. The world unhappily contains many such lost souls. They are often in high places, men trained to manipulate the machinery of civilization but utterly incapable of handling their own purposes in any civilized fashion, for their purposes are merely the relics of an infancy when their wishes were law, and they knew neither necessity nor change.[1]

Education is man's attempt to know what he is by knowing both what he can achieve and on what he ultimately depends. This self-awareness means a consciousness of both psychological strengths and weaknesses; awareness of social roles as parent and citizen; awareness of the interrelations of the governments and labor unions and business and industry; awareness of the forces that make for productivity or self-development or moral virtue; awareness of the nature of culture. Impulsive reactions to an environment ought, with the

1. Walter Lippman, *A Preface to Morals* (New York: Macmillan, 1929), pp. 183–84.

achievement of emotional maturity, to give way to informed, accurate, and deliberate actions. Sensitivity to more than merely rhythm should characterize one's sympathy for music. The eye should be a gate for more than photographic reality in the presence of the visual arts. And loyalty to institutions and persons should be one's personal responsiveness in love and generosity.

A second outcome of education, as we have said, should be a continual involvement with books. The intelligent and habitual use of books provides an access to facts, ideas, and aesthetic experiences available in no other way. Certainly this involvement with books should not eliminate other aesthetic experiences communicated by sight and sound in the arts. Nevertheless books remain the basic tools of the educated man. They are his special concern as substance for the life of the mind.

A third outcome should be the habit of accuracy. Whether one is trained as an engineer, architect, historian, or poet, accuracy is an essential quality. It begins with the simplicities of spelling, pronunciation, and the use of numbers. It continues to the selection of appropriate words and on to the more profound problem of the psychological orientation to expressing the truth. If there be anything of good report, if there be any virtue, any praise in studies for the Ph.D., it is just at this point. At the graduate level, if no other, it is an education in accuracy.

Emotional maturity, continual involvement with books, and the habit of accuracy point toward two other qualities that educated men and women should possess.

One is a reflective mind. It was Pascal who said, "Thought makes the whole dignity of man; therefore endeavor to think well." To follow Pascal's counsel and "think well" requires a clear sense of importance, meaning, or value. It does matter, in terms of personal and social development, whether we learn to think in relation to subjects that have greater or less intrinsic significance.

The reflective mind, given to deliberation, will look for the premises as well as at the structure of the argument. It will entertain opposing theses with calm dispassion. It will evaluate the interrelationships of means and ends, aware that forms of procedure do not necessarily determine ends and certainly are not to be confused with them.

The reflective mind is eager to be well informed, to have all the facts, not just those that lie on the surface. The reflective mind has respect for the knowledge of the past because it is aware of the great lesson of history, that those who do not know the blunders of the past are condemned to repeat them. The reflective mind, however, looks forward as well as backward. In a rapidly changing world it is deeply concerned with foresight and the emerging shape of the future.

And finally, the reflective mind is concerned with decision and action. "The art of life," said Mr. Justice Holmes, "consists in making correct decisions on insufficient evidence." Life does not permit perpetually suspended judgment. Werner Jaeger made a great advance in Aristotelian study by establishing the originality of that philosopher in his distinction of the practical intellect (phronesis) and the contemplative intellect (sophia) or wisdom. The reflective mind, although akin to Aristotle's contemplative intellect, is not one that cannot be made up. Indeed free men must act. A slave is a being who habitually submits to having his choices made for him by some other man. The very nature of a dynamic society is such that if a man does not decide himself, history will decide for him. For the educated man action or decision is preceded, not pre-

vented, by thought. All too often people forget to engage the
gears of the mind before stepping on the gas both figuratively
and physically. There are times when one feels like crying out
as did Demosthenes to the Athenians, "In God's name, I beg
of you to think!"

A fifth outcome of education should be an ever-widen-
ing range of curiosity. The specialist is only half educated if he is
only a specialist. The old box camera without a lens provided
a rather narrow limit of focus. The 35 mm camera was a vast
improvement upon this. The educated man should look on life
with a collection of refined lenses ranging from the close-up
portrait to the extended telephoto but especially the wide
angle. His universe of concern should be an expanding universe, as is that in which he lives.

These five outcomes suggest an old Greek definition
of happiness as one suitable to describe education: "The exercise of vital powers along lines of excellence in a life affording
them scope."[2]

Now these five—emotional maturity, continual involvement with books, the habit of accuracy, a reflective mind, and
a widening range of curiosity—point one step further. Alfred
North Whitehead reminds us that "apart from some transcendent aim the civilized life either wallows in pleasure or relapses
into a barren repetition with waning intensities of feeling."[3]
This is what was meant by the ancient proverb in Scripture:
"Where there is no vision the people perish."[4]

2. Quoted in Edith Hamilton, *The Greek Way to Western
Civilization* (New York: Mentor, 1958), p. 21.

3. Alfred North Whitehead, *Adventures of Ideas* (New York:
Macmillan, 1933), p. 108.

4. Proverbs 29:18.

Certain periods of human history, quite apart from favorable political or economic circumstances, indeed sometimes amid the most apparently unfavorable conditions, turn out to be times of enormous cultural productivity. Other times are arid and poor. Close scrutiny has not yet revealed the mystery of this grace of productivity beyond disclosing that at each such time there were individuals possessed of a deeper vision of ultimate reality than most of their fellows, persons consequently of new faith and stronger wings for action.

Athens presents such a case. Edith Hamilton opens her volume *The Greek Way* with these words:

> Five hundred years before Christ in a little town on the far western border of the settled and civilized world, a strange new power was at work. Something had awakened in the minds and spirits of the men there, which was so to influence the world that the slow passage of long time, of century upon century, and the shattering changes they brought would be powerless to wear away that deep impress. Athens had entered upon her belief and magnificent flowering of genius. The Greeks were the first intellectualists. In a world where the irrational had played the chief role, they came forward as the protagonists of the mind. . . . Men were thinking for themselves.[5]

The vital element in civilization is this quality that cannot itself be learned—"inspiration," "vision," "a transcendent aim." Call it what we will, but find it we must if we aspire to the uncommon life.

5. Hamilton, *The Greek Way*, pp. 7, 10–11.

9

Knowledge Crowns Those
Who Seek Her

A T ITS HIGHEST AND BEST, education is the intellectual
and moral development of the perfect prince. It is the
training of the wise and good ruler, be his name
Caesar, King, or citizen in a country truly free.

As Plato remarks in the fifth book of the *Republic*:
"Until philosophers are kings, or the kings and princes of this
world have the spirit and power of philosophers, and political
greatness and wisdom meet in one, . . . cities will never have
rest from their evils." Plato was not successful in his efforts
in ancient Syracuse as tutor to Dionysius II, who at the age of
thirty had become the reigning tyrant. Nor are we likely to be
successful as we attempt to improve city, state, and federal
government. Nevertheless, this is what we should try to do.
Plato was right. The goal of the American school and college
is the education of the perfect prince or princess. We accept
this as the goal for all the people, since all hold royal power,
all are both citizens and rulers. How well we succeed determines the level of our culture, the strength of our nation, and

the organization of the world for prosperity and peace: *Suos Cultores Scientia Coronat.*[1]

The classical revival made a deep mark on Upstate New York. Its villages and cities bear such names as Homer, Rome, Tully, Utica, Apulia, Troy, Hector, Cicero, Marcellus, Marathon, and Syracuse. Where communities bear such names there was nothing incongruous about a university motto that borrows the image of a prince not yet crowned. It was characteristic in that age of faith to understand that education is the key to power and that there is no royal crown more significant than the crown of knowledge. Those who selected the motto of Syracuse University were ambitious, but they were nonetheless simple, old-fashioned, God-fearing people. They selected a dead language because that was the language of the learned man. They liked the imagery of kings and crowned heads, but they betrayed their agricultural origins by using the word *cultores*. To be sure they did not use the term "agriculture"—the culture of the fields—but the meaning is the same. It is the figure of the man with a plough turning over the soil, a man drenched with sweat from the hardest kind of toil. Even when translated into the labor of a student it is work such as Goethe had in mind when he wrote that no one knows the meaning of work "whose bread hath ne'er been steeped in tears."[2] "*Suos Cultores*" is not a dilettante phrase. It is earthy, honest, and straight from the farm.

Scientia is a more modern and more controversial

1. The motto of Syracuse University, "Knowledge Crowns Those Who Seek Her."

2. Johann Wolfgang Von Goethe, *William Meister's Apprenticeship*, trans. by R. Dillon Boylan (London: Bell, 1875), Book II, p. 122.

word. One wonders why it was chosen rather than *sophia*—wisdom, or *veritas*—truth. Its selection is something of a surprise. In general the world has been critical of *scientia*. This is the theoretical and philosophical knowledge of the intellect. This is the book-knowledge of the classroom and study, the product of the library and the science laboratory. It is the life of the mind. This is the peculiar business of a school or college. This is what distinguishes an educational institution from a church, a reform school, a hospital, a country club, a YMCA or a YWCA. There is no point in being defensive about it. Whether a college succeeds or not depends on what it does about *scientia*.

Suos Cultores Scientia Coronat. To those who toil at this business—to those who work hard enough, to those who never cease to seek *scientia*—the reward is like the coronation of a king or of a queen. Commencement exercises are a kind of coronation. They are the democratic counterpart of an honors list at court. The work that earns an Associate degree, a Baccalaureate, a Master's, or a Doctorate is a progressive honors list, with varying degrees of nobility like the range from baronet to duke.

This, however, is a time of change. Even royal families are now insecure. The laurel of Apollo no longer guards the gates of the Caesars. Heredity alone no longer insures a throne. The right to rule must be earned again in each generation. This is true even in the democracies of the citizen rulers.

In knowledge, too, this is a new world, and the explosion of new knowledge is under way. We wonder how the members of a graduating class would react if the commencement speaker said "I regret to inform you that what you have learned is now obsolete."

It is not completely true, but there is too much truth

in it for comfort. Moreover there is nothing any of us can do about it but to continue to update our education. Generations before could think of themselves as heirs of a magnificent past with enough intellectual capital so all could live on the income of it. Not so today. The past is still important, but it is no longer enough. The rate of change is too rapid. Tomorrow's demands will be very different from today's. Only with tomorrow's knowledge can we understand tomorrow's world.

Thus, the all-important questions are: will we keep on learning? Will we keep on seeking *scientia*? Can we still be described as *suos cultores*? In the world of tomorrow we will go to school in some sense as long as we live. There are some forty million Americans taking adult education courses of one kind or another, and the number grows greater each year. More than 50 percent of those taking Baccalaureate degrees will go on to graduate or professional schools. Graduate work is already more common than undergraduate work was a generation ago.

The great emphasis of our time is on vocational or professional development. The young engineer knows that in order to keep up with his field he must continue his studies. The scientist, the teacher, the lawyer, and the doctor feel the same pressures. And now the young business executive is learning that what applies to the professional man applies also to him.

The pressures of a competitive society may take care of continuing education in our chosen vocation or profession. There is, however, no evidence of any like pressure to cultivate our private intellectual life. This will not be cultivated unless we feel strongly about it and continue to feel that way. This is a period when all of our communication media and our cultural influences tend to make us more and more alike. There is increasing homogeneity of attitudes, opinions, tastes, and consumption patterns. Yet if education has taught us anything it is that each of us is an individual, with his or her unique image. Moreover, if we do our own thinking we shall not think alike.

So the pressures of our day are to be resisted. Thinking is rare. Even the habit of reading good books is rare. The late Henry Mencken in a particularly cynical mood once declared: "Most men don't think thirty minutes in their whole lifetime. Any man who can think two minutes at a stretch is a genius."

Most of us will hear good music, will go to the theatre and enjoy it, will visit museums and keep up in some degree with changes in art. We shall probably also do our share of travel. What is more doubtful is how much poetry we will read, how much philosophy, how much science, how many forgotten classics, how much fiction and nonfiction not on the list of best sellers.

Will we read regularly and with enjoyment books that feed the mind, that open new doors of understanding that throw light on complex issues, that rub away our prejudices and compel us to revise our views? Will we continue the building of our personal library with increasing discrimination and pleasure?

Richard Jeffries reminds us, "It is the peculiarity of knowledge that those who really thirst for it always get it." This makes it sound easy. The truth, however, is that everything in our busy Western life conspires against the cultivation of the private intellectual life.

Even among the literate there is a preoccupation with the latest fashions in thought and a singular unwillingness to challenge what Mill calls "the received opinions." Howard

Mumford Jones reminds us that if one should inquire, as Crevecoeur did in 1832, "who is this new man in America," the answer would often be "he is a lonely soul lost in the wilderness of neo-Calvinism and midnight melancholy." But there is also the emptiness of life bounded by bridge and golf games, soap operas, and comic books. If there is a cure, we should find it in a wider and a deeper intellectual life. The life of the mind must be fed and exercised. It also needs a balanced diet. The mind does not continue to grow when left to itself.

In *Philosopher's Holiday* Irwin Edman tells of his experience over a period of years with a young sailor named Jewell. Professor Edman had introduced the sailor to Wagner's Meistersinger. In attempting to describe the music, the sailor referred to the Gospel of St. John: "Remember what he says about the Word become Flesh? It's a wonderful phrase and it tells a lot about writing. The Word became Flesh. Some writing is that. Touched with flame, certain writing is. The spirit become incarnate. You can tell at once the real thing from the fake. That Wagner music has it: touched with flame."[3]

Professor Edman had his failures as well as his successes with students. At the close of his essay he notes with sadness: "Jewell has been married some years now. There is a little boy who bears the writer's name. Jewell seems happy, though less exuberantly than of old, and he finds it difficult, he tells me when I see him, to keep up with ideas now. 'And philosophical ideas don't seem such cures for the world as I

3. Irwin Edman, *Philosopher's Holiday* (New York: Viking, 1938), p. 51.

used to think,' he said, 'not the world I see around me on shore and read about in the papers.' "[4]

"I gathered," concludes Professor Edman, "that on a milkman's wages and with a wife to support and a child to bring up, things in general are not touched with flame, nor is ecstasy as obvious any more."[5]

That is the problem, whether we are milkmen or housewives or business or professional people. What do we do about our education when things in general are not touched with flame, and ecstasy is not obvious any more?

The quality of our culture is revealed by the things we honor by our interests, our dollars, and our energies. If we are mindful of professional development and the private intellectual life, what about the duties of the citizen, the sense of social responsibility of the educated man? If education is the training of a prince, is not this of the highest importance?

The beautiful words of the Athenian Oath remind us, "We will ever strive for the ideals and sacred things of the City, both alone and with many. We will increasingly seek to quicken the sense of public duty; we will revere and obey the city's laws; we will transmit this City not only less, but greater, better and more beautiful than it was transmitted to us."

In a democracy the education of a prince is the education of the citizen. The mission of the school, the college, and the university is in part the education of the future ruler. If we really understood this, it is inconceivable that the course of study would be science alone or humanities alone. The study

4. Ibid., p. 52.

5. Ibid., p. 53.

of public affairs, the understanding of our legal and political system, the complex issues of domestic and foreign policy, are central and continuing interests. Because we are citizen-rulers we cannot plead indifference or flee from responsibility. Because we are responsible we must keep ourselves informed.

One of the watchwords of our time is freedom. We should like all men to be free. It is not simply freedom, however, that has made the United States great. It is freedom with responsibility. We cannot divorce the two. The college graduate who has not taken seriously his duties as a citizen should begin now. There is much to learn. There is no time to wait. Yet, we should remember the caveat of Woodrow Wilson, "The fault of our age is the fault of hasty action, of premature judgments, or of a preference for ill-considered action over no action at all. . . . We see an error, and we hastily correct it by a greater error and then go on to cry that the age is corrupt."

Education for public affairs appears to be that part of the mind where logic and common sense count least. The saddest feature of American democracy is the failure of its citizens to understand what government cannot do even with all the money in this world. The future of democratic government is bleak indeed without better education for individual responsibility and governmental accountability.

To those who weigh and consider, to those who reflect and reason, life is a seamless robe in which both values and facts are threads. Character and scholarship are not two things. Rightly conceived they are one. Good scholarship demands honesty and reverence for truth. Our approach to knowledge must have the integrity of the scientist and the scholar.

We are conservators of a tradition that goes back to

Homer. What do we conserve? Certainly it is not the answers, though the trail blazed in a wilderness of conflicting counsel is one all wise men will follow. Certainly it is not beliefs, though some have held the world together. Certainly it is not the findings of science, important as it is to keep the record of man's scientific inquiry.

We are conservators of the spirit of learning, of the place of freedom, of respect for reason, and of reverence for the search for truth. The question is whether we are strong enough to continue our learning without the lure of degrees, without the requirement of credits, without the supervision of teachers, without the paternalism and fraternalism of deans and professors and fellow students.

The late Charles C. Noble, Dean of Hendricks Chapel at Syracuse University, defined education as a love affair with truth; a love affair with knowledge and wisdom. It is a good definition—and Dean Noble gave it deeper meaning by reminding us that we cannot take such a love affair for granted. We must continue the courtship, continue the wooing.

Plato in one of his letters expresses some doubts as to whether we can explain what we mean by the word *philosophy*. "There does not exist, and there never shall, any treatise by myself on these matters. The subject does not admit as the sciences do, of exposition." Then follow these luminous words, which describe the meaning of education as well as philosophy. "It is only after long association in the great business itself and a shared life that a light breaks out in the soul, kindled, so to say, by a leaping flame, and thereafter feels itself."[6]

6. *The Works of Plato*, edited by Irwin Edman (New York: Simon and Schuster, 1928), p. xiv.

Has a light been kindled in the soul? Will the leaping flame continue to be fed by the soul's hungers and ambitions? Will we commit ourselves to service beyond self, to magnanimity and brotherhood, and to the search for goodness and truth that leads us to the Divine Source? Is this love affair with knowledge one that will endure?

In our active seeking for new knowledge we do not cease to be the conservators of the age-old quest for righteousness and wisdom. New answers do not halt the search for knowledge. New insights, broader views, fresh discoveries are welcome despite the havoc to prejudice and the conventional wisdom.

We cannot tell what we shall become. We do not know whether we can do all that is expected of us. All we know is that it is not beyond our reach. It is not impossible. It is, in fact, what we must take as our clear objective, our announced goal. Knowledge gives the laurel wreath to those who seek her. This is the crown we should resolve to win!

10

No Ordinary Bird

THE BOOK *Jonathan Livingston Seagull* begins with these words:

It was morning and the new sun sparkled gold across the ripples of a gentle sea. . . . .

Way off alone, out by himself beyond boat and shore Jonathan Livingston Seagull was practicing. A hundred feet in the sky he lowered his webbed feet, lifted his beak and strained to hold a painful twisting curve through his wings. The curve meant that he would fly slowly, and now he slowed until the wind was a whisper in his face, until the ocean stood still beneath him. He narrowed his eyes in fierce concentration, held his breath, forced one-single-more-inch of curve. Then his feathers ruffled, he stalled and fell.

Seagulls, as you know, never falter, never stall. To stall in the air is for them disgrace and it is dishonor.

But Jonathan Livingston Seagull—unashamed, stretching his wings again in that trembling hard curve-slowing, slowing, and stalling once more—was no ordinary bird.[1]

Like Jonathan Livingston Seagull, people deeply interested in the pursuit of learning are no ordinary birds. We pay no ordinary price in effort, practice, study, and self-denial. The pursuit of learning is not easy.

William James used to say that if he could preach only one sermon he would choose the text from the Second Chapter of Ezekiel: "Son of Man, stand upon they feet and I will speak to thee."

James believed that the proper posture for man was to stand erect, to stand with pride, resolved to do his full part in life. He believed that God helps most those who help themselves.

I like the text William James chose—but if I had a similar choice my text would be from the Seventh Chapter of St. Matthew: "Strait is the gate and narrow is the way which leadeth unto life and few there be that find it."

There is an old saying of the Greeks that the beautiful is hard.[2] Good workmanship is rare; perfection in art is rarer still. The beautiful is hard to create, hard to judge, and hard to preserve. A cathedral that required three hundred years to build can be destroyed in an instant by a nuclear bomb. One of the many tragedies of war and the acts of terrorist groups is the destruction of irreplaceable art—the accumulation of centuries.

1. R. Bach, *Jonathan Livingston Seagull* (New York: Macmillan, 1970; Avon, 1973), pp. 11–12.

2. Κάλεπα τὰ καλά. "Hard is the good." Plato, *The Republic*, Book VI. *The Dialogues of Plato*, edited by Benjamin Jowett (New York: Charles Scribner's Sons, 1890), Vol. II, p. 324.

Truth is also hard. It, too, is difficult to discover, difficult to judge, difficult to keep. Painfully made discoveries in the arts and sciences were lost in the decline and fall of early civilizations. Many arts and technical processes known to earlier cultures are still unknown to us today.

Truth is as elusive as mercury. Much that passed as science yesterday is fiction today. Much that was called truth is now regarded as superstition. Many of the things that seemed most certain are now but old wives' tales.

In some fields truth is particularly hard to find. The discussion of justice in Plato's *Republic* illustrates the difficulty of the quest for truth in the field of political science and human relations. We make constant use of abstract ideas like justice, goodness, and wisdom. How many conflicting definitions there are! Who among us can define them in terms that would win universal assent?

The New Testament suggests that there is also nothing easy about goodness. It, too, is difficult to define. It is difficult to judge, difficult to win, and difficult to keep. "It is a strait gate and a narrow way."

L. P. Jacks reminds us:

when we examine the mysterious thing called "Life" there is one deeply interesting and significant fact which can hardly fail to provoke our wonder. All the activities of life operated in the face of opposition and cannot operate otherwise. Whether a government can be carried on without an opposition, remains to be seen; but life without opposition is not to be found anywhere. All of life's activities, physical, mental, moral and spiritual, and the last no less than the first, do their work in a resisting medium, and need it if they are to go on at all.

Every living thing is an example of this. The bird needs the resisting medium of the air to fly; the fish of the water to swim; and man when he stands upright is resisting a tendency to fall, though he may be unconscious of it. Standing upright might be defined as successful resistance to the force of gravitation.

So, too, when we turn to the sphere of our moral activities and study the man who is standing upright in the moral sense. He, too, is resisting a tendency to fall in another way, though he may be doing so unconsciously.

Morality always functions in a resisting medium. The "good life," takes what form it may, is never a "walk over," never an operation performed in a vacuum.

Whatever aspect of human life we examine, from the physical to the spiritual, the same conditions confront us. Every form of it represents a victory won over a resisting medium of one kind or another. Our common habits of decency are victories won over corresponding indecencies; our civilization is a victory won over error, and our logic is a weapon for fighting our tendency to make mistakes.[3]

James Hinton reminds us that "little inconveniences, exertions, pains,—there are the only things in which we rightly feel our life at all. If these be not there, existence becomes worthless, or worse; success in putting them all away is fatal. So it is men engage in athletic sports, spend their holidays in climbing up mountains, and find nothing so enjoyable as that which taxes their endurance and their energy. This is the way we are made, I say. It may or may not be a mystery or a paradox; it is a fact."

3. Lawrence Pearsall Jacks, *The Revolt Against Mechanism*, (New York: Macmillan, 1934), pp. 19–24.

The good is hard in every field of knowledge. Whether our goal is music, art, literature, or science, we succeed only by exceptional dedication and effort. Paderewski practiced every day and every evening until late at night and did hours of stretching exercises for his short fingers that could barely reach an octave. He lived in stark poverty. His only son was a cripple, never able to walk. He lost his deeply beloved wife. But as the hero of his nation and greatest musician of his time he could still say: "You must accept your suffering in order to be urged on toward your ascent."[4]

Paderewski tells us in his autobiography:

> It took half of my life, to realize that there are two ways of using the piano. The one is to play, the other is to work. If you use the one, you will never achieve anything. You are carried away with your own emotions and with the emotion of the contents of the work you are playing. And you might spend the whole of your life in playing without learning anything. *You can be drunk in any art on your own emotions.* And, alas, a great many people are wasting their time that way, arriving at no results at all. While working of course, you suffer, because you have absolutely no pleasure, only effort and pain.[5]

Malvina Hoffman, whose "Hall of Man" in the Field Museum at Chicago is one of America's important contributions to art, echoes the same sentiment in her book, *Heads and*

4. Ignace Jan Paderewski and Mary Lawton, *The Paderewski Memoirs* (New York: Charles Scribner's Sons, 1935).

5. Ibid.

Tales. She is too modest to do any boasting but we learn that before she became a sculptor she spent years perfecting her accuracy in drawing and modeling, studied human anatomy by dissection, studied carpentry, learned to make and repair her own tools, learned how to build wood and iron armatures, and how to cast her own bronzes. She forced herself to master half a dozen trades. It was typical of her thoroughness that she was unwilling to make a frieze of Pavlowa's "Autumn Bacchanale" until she herself had learned this dance from start to finish. She had made at least a hundred drawings of Pavlowa at rehearsals and had been watching the Russian dancers for months, but it was only when she herself had experienced the full ecstasy of the dance that she felt ready to depict it on bas-relief.

In her autobiography *Yesterday is Tomorrow*, she refers to a winter of uninterrupted work on eight pieces of sculpture and then observes: "People don't understand that you have to work so hard and there are no short cuts. If there are, although I've lived rather long, I have never found any. I have to work my way to knowledge, and there never seems any other way to get it."[6]

As we turn our attention to our future, the all-important question is our continuing growth and, as we grow older, our self-renewal. Our formal schooling is designed to help us become all that we are capable of becoming. In the years after school we should continue to grow. Life is the art of becoming.

6. Malvina Hoffman, *Yesterday is Tomorrow* (New York: Crown, 1965), p. 340.

Don M. Wolfe notes that "each new experience of high school or college opportunities represents an investment in perhaps the most fundamental of all unproved assumptions on the American scene; that children and adults are more plastic and malleable in their response to books, teachers, and ideas than any scientist has yet suspected."[7] This does not mean, however, that education will make us equal. Animals are not equal. Men are not equal. Equality of educational opportunity simply gives all the same opportunity.

The productivity of men differs even more than the productivity of cows. Genetic differences are enormous in the same family. The Parable of the Talents recognizes the inequality of men, but we pretend that we would all be equal if we had the same advantages. Christopher Jencks has made himself unpopular by reporting the evidence to the contrary.

We know more about genetic differences in farm animals than of genetic differences in farmers. We apply more sense to the breeding of animals than we do to the marriage selection process of men. It is important to know the ways in which animals and men are alike. It is even more important, however, to know the ways in which they are different.

The first difference is that man is unfinished at birth. As Professor William Ernest Hocking says, "Of all beings it is man in whom heredity counts for least and conscious building forces for most—other creatures nature could largely finish; the human creature must finish himself."[8]

7. Don M. Wolfe, *The Image of Man in America,* 2nd ed. (New York: Crowell, 1970), pp. 431–32.

8. William Ernest Hocking, *Human Nature and Its Remaking* (New Haven: Yale University Press, 1918), pp. 15–16.

Man is the most helpless of newborn animals. He has the longest infancy. He is less dependent on instincts, more dependent on the use of his mind and with unique powers of habit-making and habit-changing. It takes him longer to mature physically. Even when his legs begin to grow old and he has passed the peak of his physical powers, he is still unfinished in the development of his mental and spiritual powers. We should note, however, that the aging of the body and the decay of spirit and mind are closely related to their care, their exercise, their use. What is not developed is slowly but surely lost. Nature takes away whatever we do not use. Regardless of age, however, we are remarkably free to continue our learning and self-realization.

The second difference is that man is a citizen of two worlds: the world of body and the world of mind, the world of matter and the world of spirit, the world of necessity and the world of freedom. In a more limited sense this may also be true of some animals. We should be slow to belittle intelligence and instinct in animals.

I remember a summer in Canada when I had purchased fifty green frogs and brought them to our camp in Georgian Bay. They were in a large bucket, and before going to bed I had put the bucket in the kitchen at the back of the cottage. In the middle of the night I was awakened by a curious scratching sound against the screens on the front porch. The frogs had escaped and, following their instincts, were trying to make their way through the cottage toward the world of water the cottage faced. They were demonstrating that they are citizens of two worlds—the world of land and the world of water.

Man too depends on instinct, but he is also moved by

words and ideas. They can run in his head like a fever. He is influenced by hopes, dreams, ideals, ambitions, and aspirations. He lives by values and by faith.

The third difference between men and animals grows out of the first two. Man is an unfinished animal with the capacity to learn as long as he lives. As a citizen of two worlds, we cannot put a ceiling on his development. Nor can we limit the degree of control he has over his future. In the world of nature man is unique in his ability to increase his mental, physical, and spiritual powers.

To be sure, much is predetermined by heredity. Much, too, depends on diet, health, and care. The greatest difference, however, is man's response to opportunity for learning, his response to the influence of books and teachers, and his capacity for self-motivation, self-discipline, and self-direction.

There is an old saying, "Young man, be very careful about what you want from life, for almost certainly you will get it." The saying is true. The goal we build our life about, we are likely to get, whether it is money, political influence, eminence in a profession, or a life of unselfish service. We must choose carefully, for we may not like what we get.

To a surprising degree, assuming an opportunity for education, we can write our own travel ticket. What we want most, work hard for, and make substantial sacrifices to achieve is seldom beyond reach. Man is the only animal with the ability to choose his own goals and with the power to move toward them. He confounds all the skeptics about the limits of growth and development. Even with equal opportunity we are not equal; however, we are all malleable. We are all capable of astonishing growth in skills, knowledge, and power if we will pay the price in self-discipline and toil. Some of us come closer than others in realizing our potential, but all of us have a higher ceiling than we reach. In the process from *posse* to *esse*, what is actual is but a part of what was and is possible.

One of the problems of Western society is its low view of man. It is a view of man as an animal, amoral and without faith. It is an incomplete view, an inadequate view. And a large part of it is because of the kind of models we have chosen to emulate. To achieve excellence we must have a vision of excellence. To achieve greatness we must have models of greatness.

Not too long ago there was a widely syndicated newspaper and radio series under the title, "Man is What He Eats." It had a high view of food and a low view of man. Food will make us fat. It will also keep us alive, but we are more than what we eat.

Perhaps a better thesis would have been, "Man is What He Reads." Certainly few things make so great a difference. The habit of reading widely gives life new dimensions and ensures growth and self-renewal. The diet of the mind either arrests or accelerates our mental development. It is clear that man is shaped by what he sees, what he hears, what he does, what he thinks, and what he aspires to be. "As a man thinketh in his heart, so is he."

Everyone who has spent his life with students should be an optimist about human nature and, with a few crossed fingers, about human society. Each year we witness the miracle of change and growth. Each year reinforces our faith in the value and importance of the learning experience.

There is much truth in the dreams of youth. We do need to aim high, to hitch our wagons to a star. In all the studies of bright young people that follow them through life, what appears to make the greatest difference is the level of their aspiration.

In his poem "The Road Not Taken," Robert Frost said,

> Two roads diverged in a wood and I took
> the one less travelled by and that has
> made all the difference.[9]

Browning put it in his own inspiring words: "The aim, if reached or not, makes great the life," and again, "And a man's reach should exceed his grasp, or what's a heaven for?"[10]

We can become what we want to become. We have enormous freedom and power in the art of becoming.

We began with the opening words of *Jonathan Livingston Seagull*. Let us close with the final paragraph: "And though he tried to look properly severe for his students, Fletcher Seagull suddenly saw them all as they really were, just for a moment, and he more than liked, he loved what he saw. No limits, Jonathan? he thought, and he smiled. His race to learn had begun."

Let each of us resolve that our race to learn has begun. Life is learning. Learning is the art of becoming.

9. Robert Frost, *Collected Poems*, "The Road Not Taken" (New York: Henry Holt, 1939), p. 131.

10. Robert Browning, *The Works of Robert Browning*, "Andrea del Sarto" (New York: Ams Press, 1966), Vol. IV, p. 120.

11

A Promethean Faith

ONE OF THE MOST INTERESTING PLAYS of Ancient Greece is *Prometheus Bound* by Aeschylus. As a play it presents some special problems to a director. There is no formal introduction. It assumes that the audience is familiar with the whole story. It is, in fact, as if we were beginning with the second act. Again there is very little dramatic action and there is no change of scenery. There is nothing contemporary about it. It is clearly a play from a distant time. It does not deal with ordinary people. The language is far from ordinary, with an almost liturgical quality, and with the sweetest music in the words.

Zeus is discouraged with the race of men. He determines to destroy mankind and try something better. Thus he withholds certain gifts more appropriate for divinity than wretched and weak creatures like men. Among these is the gift of fire.

Moved by pity for man, Prometheus steals some embers, and man, with this new help from heaven, discovers art after art, lifting his status until even Zeus sees that man is too strong to be destroyed.

Zeus is checkmated. Prometheus, however, must pay the penalty. In challenging the power and will of Zeus, he has threatened the whole moral and religious base of society. Excuse him if you will, but he is guilty of unbridled self-assertion (hubris). Moreover, he is unwilling to repent. He must, therefore, pay the price.

As punishment, Prometheus is to be chained to a rock by Hephaestus and consigned to Hades. Nor is this all. Hermes, bringing a message from Zeus, tells him that he will be tortured daily by an eagle feasting on his liver. The liver will grow by night as fast as the eagle consumes it by day. Thus the torture will continue until some god voluntarily takes the place of Prometheus in Hades.

The play ends with a thunderbolt from heaven which strikes the rock to which Prometheus is chained and sinks it to Hades.

The name of Prometheus is honored as the founder and savior of human civilization. It is the Promethean spirit of challenge, invention, creativity, and courage that explains the glory of man and the wonders of human progress.

Prometheus tells the story in these words:

. . . let me speak
Of the miseries of men, helpless children till
I gave them sense and ways to think . . .
Though I do not mention man through any blame
But only to unfold the love with which I gave.
Those first had eyes to see, but never saw;
Ears for hearing, but they never heard.
Like huddled shapes in dreams, they used to drag
Their long lives through, confusing all:

Knew no brick-built homes to front the sun,
No woodwork; but beneath the soil
They lived like tiny ants recessed in sunless holes;
No measured sign for winter, flowery spring,
Nor summer full of fruit;
Without a clue they practiced everything,
Until I showed the stars to them,
Their rising and their set—
So difficult to calculate.
And numbers, too, I found them,
The key to sciences;
And letters in their synthesis—
Secret of all memory, sweet mother of the arts.
I was the first to break beasts to the yoke
And bring them to the collar and the saddle,
So make them take on mankind's heaviest work.
I fixed the horse submissively to carriages:
Golden symbol of luxury and state.
And I was the one—none other—to invent
The seaman's ocean-roaming chariots with linen wings. . . .
. . . Ah! Listen to the rest; be more amazed
At all the arts I found, and all the ways,
The greatest: than when a man fell ill
There was no remedy at all,
No diet, liniment or draught. So men decayed.
To skeletons for lack of drugs,
Until I showed them how to mix emollient recipes,
So keep away from all disease.
. . . So much for these.
Now come to human blessings hidden in the earth:
Brass, iron, silver, gold . . .
Who claims he uncovered these before me?
. . . The whole truth in a sentence, if you want it short,
Is: Every art to man Prometheus brought. (440–506)

Schools and colleges are Promethean institutions. They too have brought every art to man. They have the Promethean faith in man. They have the Promethean courage and hope. Like Prometheus they look forward to the distant future, sustained by their vision of what some day mankind can be. They are not afraid of the human mind. They are not afraid of the new discoveries of science. They are determined to discover more. They are not afraid of change. They welcome it. They are not afraid of freedom. In their accent on intellectual inquiry, nothing is immune from investigation and study. There are no forbidden subjects, no forbidden books. If this is a dangerous course, so be it. Schools and colleges will face the danger and assume the risks.

This Promethean faith is far from universally shared. It runs counter to the mood of many of our leading writers. It is in conflict with the pessimism of the neo-orthodox in theology. Its view of man and society is unlike the fashionable slogans of fear and anxiety. It is at variance with the spirit of self-distrust which has been so characteristic of the twentieth-century intellectual. It proclaims a faith in man lost for almost a generation; a faith which must be reaffirmed if we are to cure the world of its present malaise.

As we enter the third century of the American Dream there are many who no longer believe in our economic growth and would check it if they could. They do not understand that without it half the world will remain poor, sick, and hungry. Again many of the people who speak so feelingly of improving the lot of the little man by more governmental spending appear to regard all business growth as evil. They would kill the goose that lays the golden eggs of jobs and dollars that are taxed.

Is it not a paradox that with every achievement of man

critics are still so pessimistic about him? And has not the time
come to balance accounts and take a more Promethean view?
One of the most important problems of both philosophy and
religion is to frame a more adequate view of man and the
world.

We desire no oversimplified view of the world or of
man and his problems. This is indeed an imperfect world. It is,
however, a world that has come a long way. And it is a world
for which we still have hope.

The late Anton Carlson of the University of Chicago
took what I think is a balanced view and still preserved his
faith in man.

> As I see it, ours is not an age of science. Men are still
> driven by greed and confused by guile, rather than guided
> by reason based on our expanding knowledge. . . .
> Whether science and the scientific method, whether un-
> derstanding, honesty, reason, and justice can contrive
> survival values equal, if not superior, to the blind forces
> of nature which shaped man's past is as yet in the laps of
> the gods. Still, we cannot deny the possibility, and we
> will nurse the hope that the hairy ape who somehow lost
> his tail, grew a brain worth having, built speech and song
> out of a hiss and a roar, and stepped out of the cave to
> explore and master the universe may some day conquer
> his own irrational and myopic behavior toward his kin.

Albert Einstein had a simple but inelegant way of de-
scribing the problem of learning. He said: "You can't scratch
if you don't itch."

To define education as the business of making people

uncomfortable leaves many important things unsaid. Nevertheless, it is true that we learn most readily and quickly when we are made uncomfortable, when we are forced to use our mind. We begin to think and to learn when we are bothered by a problem we have not solved, a question we have not been able to answer, a mystery we would like to understand, a compelling need we desire to meet.

What complicates the problem of education in our time is that it must be education for change. The kind of world in which we will have our careers may differ in important respects from the world as it is today. A course of study deals only with the knowledge now available, with the transmission of existing knowledge. We can only speculate about what will be discovered and taught tomorrow. Where the future bears a close resemblance to the present, instruction in current knowledge is remarkably useful. But where the future differs in essential respects from the present, current knowledge is of less and less value except as a foundation for future learning.

The rapid obsolescence of knowledge forces more emphasis on habits of thinking, habits of reading, habits of seeing and hearing. We must go to school, in the sense of serious learning, as long as we live. We must learn only to find that what we have learned is not adequate. Life will be a constant adjustment to new conditions, new knowledge, new opportunities, new challenges, and new responsibilities. As Rosemary Park once remarked: "The one certain element about our future is surprise. The unexpected event may be more important than the certain and the fixed."

For a rapidly changing world we need the broadest possible educational program. We should delay specialization until we are grounded in fundamentals. The prospective journalist needs a wide background of science, social science, and the humanities as a preparation for the study of his own field. The prospective geologist needs mathematics, physics, chemistry, and biology as a condition to progress in his own specialty. How far he can go in geology depends particularly on his background in mathematics and physics. So it goes.

We are in the kind of world that requires a knowledge of the sciences and the humanities, and perhaps the region between them, which is the history and philosophy of science. The Baccalaureate degree given to a chemistry major should not be a certificate indicating ignorance of the humanities. The same degree awarded to a major in philosophy or history should not mean, as it so often has, a near absence of mathematical and scientific knowledge.

Education should deal with the whole man. Our Promethean faith is not in the mind alone but in man as a child of God, a creature with divine qualities, knowing good and evil.

Schools and colleges should minister as best they can to the needs of the whole man. They should try to inculcate integrity and honor. They should try to build character. They should attempt to protect our health. They should attempt to keep us sensitive to religious and moral values. They should try to give us concern for beauty as well as truth and goodness. And finally, they are conscious of the unmet needs of the world. They should try to teach us to be good citizens and to be socially useful.

Pericles said it in words that are as timely as they are timeless:

Unlike other cities, Athens expects every citizen to take an interest in public affairs; and, as a matter of fact, most Athenians have some understanding of public affairs. We do believe in knowledge as a guide to action; we have a power of thinking before we act, and of acting too, whereas many peoples can be full of energy if they do not think, but when they reflect they begin to hesitate. We like to make friends abroad by doing good and giving help to our neighbors; and we do this not from some calculation of self-interest but in the confidence of freedom in a frank and fearless spirit. I would have you fix your eyes upon Athens day by day, contemplate her potentiality—not merely what she is but what she has the power to be, until you become her lovers. Reflect that her glory has been built up by men who knew their duty, and had the courage to do it. Make them your examples and learn from them that the secret of happiness is freedom, and the secret of freedom, courage.[1]

1. Thucydides, Book II, 43, Pericles, *Funeral Orations.*

INDEX

THE ADVENTURE OF LEARNING

was composed in Linotype twelve-point Weiss, leaded two points,
with display type in foundry Weiss and Weiss Initials,
and printed letterpress by Joe Mann Associates, Inc.;
Smyth-sewn and bound over boards in Columbia Bayside Vellum
by Vail-Ballou Press, Inc.;
and published by

SYRACUSE UNIVERSITY PRESS
Syracuse, New York 13210

WILLIAM PEARSON TOLLEY, Chancellor Emeritus of Syracuse University, brings a lifetime of study and experience to writing *The Adventure of Learning*. Before accepting the presidency of Allegheny College in 1931 at the age of thirty (he was then the youngest college president in the nation) Dr. Tolley had been a teacher, author, and college dean. In 1942 he became Chancellor of Syracuse University, and his leadership during the next twenty-seven years brought about tremendous new learning facilities, a faculty of international stature, and many academic innovations. Chancellor Tolley's concern for the people comprising the University—faculty, students, staff, and friends—is legend, and his respect for and tireless work on behalf of human potential, in the great liberal arts tradition, have made Syracuse University one of the major private universities in the nation.

Chancellor Tolley has received thirty-five honorary degrees, in addition to an A.B. and A.M. from Syracuse University, a B.D. from Drew Theological Seminary, and an A.M. and Ph.D. from Columbia University. He is a member of the boards of numerous corporations, financial institutions, and service organizations.